INT

This book is a
working at sea, and the
during that borrowed time. It is not for snowflakes, the lily-livered or faint-hearted, and is written in keeping with my thoughts and feelings of the time.

Much of this took place in the Seventies and Eighties, and reflects the feelings and beliefs of that time. The attitudes and opinions do not reflect those of mine now that I am of a certain age; and I ask the reader to bear this in mind – and the Police.

All events in this book are true, and genuinely happened. It has not been necessary to exaggerate; as I have told thousands of friends. The names and characters in this book are real, and I have not changed any names to protect the insolent. Only first names have been used, and those mentioned will know who they are if they cough up the few quid to read this diatribe.

Whilst I was only in the Merchant Navy some ten years plus, the sea has influenced my life throughout, and it is my aim to recount some of the more significant things that have happened over the years for posterity.

The world is rapidly becoming obsessively politically correct, and soon it will be abhorrent to infer that snow is white. Political correctness was not in vogue, domestic international travel was for the privileged few, and the world was a different place then. PCs (personal computers) hadn't been invented, but Parental Control was still expected. Prime Cost and Practical Completion were both in use within the construction industry as they are nowadays.

Selma was only twenty to twenty-five years previous to these events; whilst this excuses nothing, it puts things into some perspective.

I hope my book will be a time-stamp, and recount a few tales from a time when blackboards weren't offensive. If you are easily offended, or think 'Snow White' should be called 'White Caucasian', I would suggest you return this book from whence it came, and demand your money back. If you can accept the world has changed, and was less perfect than it is now (hopefully); "read on, Macbeth".

My wife says I regurgitate all of the stories regularly, in full detail, to anyone who inadvertently gets caught listening (or not) to me. This book negates this requirement, and I will now become a selective mute.

In the meantime, we need to talk about Nigel.

References To Ships

Throughout the book there are many references to ship types and sizes, and it is necessary to give some perspective in order to imagine, and hopefully understand the scope of the vessels I sailed on. I spent more time on motor ships than steam ships i.e. large marine diesel engines versus steam turbine, and the bulk of this time on "Ity Boats" (Tenacity, Unity etc), "River Boats" (Dart, Humber, Mokran etc), and "R Boats" (Reliance, Respect etc).

"Ity" and "River" class ships were circa 25,500-ton deadweight i.e. they carried 25,500 tons of product cargo; diesel, petrol, aviation spirit etc. The ships themselves actually weighed in the region of 14,500 tons; hence when fully loaded they displaced circa 40,000 tons.

Length 171.5m   Breadth 25m   Draught 9.6m

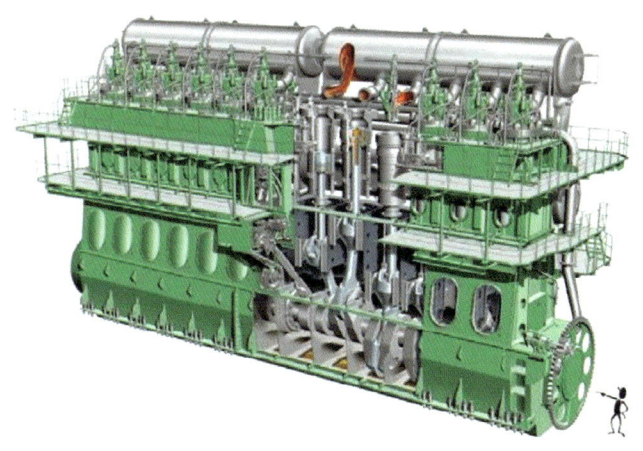

"R" class ships were circa 280,000-ton deadweight i.e. they carried 280,000 tons of crude oil. The ships themselves actually weighed in the region of 120,000 tons; hence when fully loaded they displaced in the region of 400,000 tons.

Length 382m   Breadth 55m   Draught 21m

To put these details in perspective, HMS Queen Elizabeth (our largest aircraft carrier) is 280m long and displaces 65,000 tons; one sixth the size of the VLCCs I sailed on, and Type 23 Frigates range from 2,500-4,500 tons; about a tenth the size of a River boat, or one-hundredth the size of the product carriers.

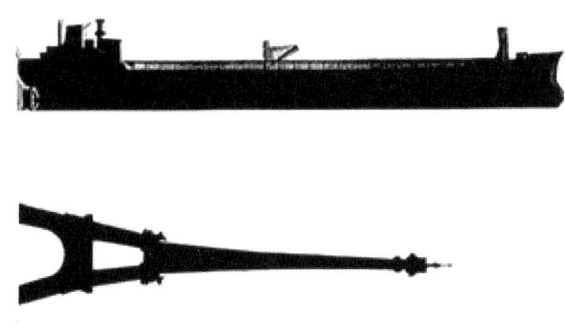

Glossary of Terms

Arrows – Darts

Ballast – Sea water loaded into empty tanks to retain ship's stability.

Big Panic House – Britannic House; BP's head office at the time

Blighty – The UK

Bronzying – Sun bathing

Coaster – A small ship which trades around the coast; as opposed to deep-sea (not a mat)

Dhobi engine – Twin-tub washing machine

Dogs nuts – rather good

Engineers blue – a blue dye compound used to check if surfaces are truly flat (stains badly!)

Fall over – In engineering terms, 'to go faulty' or malfunction

Flog the log – To guess parameters and enter them in the logbook as fact

Gizits – Presents to take home ("give us it")

Handi-matic – Manual

Hawse pipe – The pipe where the anchor sits when raised, and the chain drops through at anchor

Heads – Toilets

Itty boat – This was the term for the 24,000-ton product carriers; all with names ending in 'ity', British Tenacity, British Unity, and ironically the MV British Humber (don't ask)

Jack Tar – Sailor (from the old sailing days when the sailors used tar to tame their hair (no barbers)

Lub – lubricating oil

Niggers wad – A wad of bank notes; except the top and bottom notes sandwich blank paper (a cunning trick)

Nobby Clark – Shark

Paraffin budgie – Aeroplane

Pay off – Leaving the ship to go home at the end of a trip. This emanates from the days when the crew were only employed per trip

Pick – Anchor

Pit – The engine room

Poop deck – The aft-most deck at the stern of a ship

Product carrier – A tanker designed to carry 'products' such as paraffin, petrol, aviation spirit and the like

Pull – To pull a piston is to remove it from its cylinder (to pull a woman is quite different)

RAS – Replenishment at sea

River boat – This was the term for the 25,000-ton product carriers; all named after British rivers, British Avon, British Dart, British Esk, British Test, British Trent, British Wye etc

Sherbets – Beers

Shit handler – Ships chandler

Shite hawk – Seagull

Skiddies – Underpants

Smoko – Rest break (when we'd smoke our fags)

Sparky – Electrician

Steam queen – A person only qualified for steam-turbine driven ships (not roughty-toughty like 'motor-men)

Tenna-City Roadshow – The fond name of the ship MV British Tenacity

Turn to – Start work
Turn turtle – Capsize
VLCC – Very large crude carrier
Whirlybird – Helicopter
Yachtie – Yachtsman

WE NEED TO TALK ABOUT NIGEL

Contents

'Tis Not The Leaving Of Liverpool …. 1

Childhood 3

School & Sea Cadets 6

Learning French 11

Musical Taste 13

Plymouth CFE 15

Losing My Virginity 25

Sheep Digging 27

MV British Commodore 30

Mombasa 35

Safari 39

Jungle Village 41

Nurses Party 43

Fishing 46

SS British Reliance 50

Glasgow College 55

Leith 59

MV Mokran 64

Apprentices 70

Sivand 73

Fluorescein 76

Hawsepipes, Fog Horns and Shit Tanks	78
Concrete Boxes	82
Broken Ribs	84
Steering Ticket	87
Dinghies & Yachts	89
Eos	93
MV British Tenacity	96
Boiler Fire	99
Donkey Boiler	111
Lomé	113
Jakarta	115
Sydney	117
Christmas Nurses Party	119
Alexandria	121
MV British Dart	124
Constanta	129
MV British Wye	131
Piréas	134
Broken Toes	136
The Perfect Storm	139
SS British Respect	144
UMS	148
Tuna	151
Blackout	158

Crude Oil Spray	161
MV British Humber	163
Belfast	165
'Vittles'	166
BP Vision	172
Scavenge Fire	177
Singapore Versus Swansea	179
SS British Respect	182
Coasters	193
Coming Ashore	197
Life Ashore	200
Acknowledgements	203

'Tis Not The Leaving Of Liverpool ….

In the beginning . . . . we were stood on a steel Leviathan: the Canadian Pacific's six-hundred and forty-foot, thirty-thousand shaft horse-power, twenty-five-and-a-half thousand-ton RMS *Empress of England*. I knew not how I got there, or if I had existed prior to this moment, standing on the deck of the ship surrounded by very emotional folk waving to crowds of ants on the port side. Ropes and a myriad of coloured streamers draped between us and the ropes' bollards at Albert Dock, Liverpool. Thousands of rainbow-coloured crepe paper umbilical cords stretched between the hulk and shore, each parting as the draw of a new life pulled us away from the jetty. It was 1964 and I was three years old.

My father had decided to uproot from Bristol and emigrate to Calgary. He even offered my mother the opportunity to join him, with the two kids, if she wanted to.

Having sold most of the few things we owned, we stored the remainder in hardboard trunks in the holds, somewhere in the bowels of the ship.

So, there we were, all emotional, leaping into the great unknown, when my elder sister Karen, conveniently decided she must have a pee at the very moment the sleeping giant heaved away from her bindings, breaking our colourful ties with Blighty, and slowly lumbered into the scum of the Mersey.

My memories of the voyage are few and far between, but I do recall strolling on the top deck with my father one sunny day and looking through the door of the single mustard funnel, presumably left open by a lazy engineer! We peered down into the spider's web of pipes and machinery: absolutely fascinating for a young lad disposed to such things. I still recall my fascination of the twisted shapes of pipes and the noise of the machinery chuntering away. How was I to know that this was to be a major part of my life to come?

Apart from the odd debacle I recall little of the outward-bound voyage; a flurry of animated crew and alarms, as they tried to get the *Empress* to manoeuvre off the sandbank at Greenock, having run aground trying to do a 180º turn; getting lost in the 'heads'; being shouted at by a punter urinating into the bowl of his toilet. Through which of all the doors had I got here? And why do guys pee standing up, their golden plume jetting into toilet bowls and liberally spraying the seat? And why don't they lock the cubicle door? These things still perplex me.

Apparently this voyage took a week at sea, followed by a further three days crossing Canada on the silver rail-snake with the caboose cars, gliding across the vast expanse of Canada. Sadly, I remember nothing of this . . .

This had been my first nautical excursion, the first of many to come!

Childhood

I recall as a young child visiting my paternal grandparents. My sister and I would have to sit very still and be genteel, occasionally being let out to play and let off steam. In those days, children were seen but not heard unless spoken to directly by an adult, and then one could answer the question politely, gauging when one's audience had been exhausted.

I loved visiting my grandparents in their mobile home in Almondsbury. I was allowed to rummage through my nan's sewing basket, a four-legged box of exciting mysterious things. But the real treasures were the two medals won by her father, Captain John Gregory (1869-1933). I was fascinated by these two gongs, the Great War medal and the Mercantile Marine medal, and loved to paw over them imagining my Great Grandfather on his ship *Cato* (1914-1940). Then during a visit, my Nan showed me the contents of an envelope, tantalisingly left in the sewing box: an original photograph of the *Cato* chugging up the Avon Gorge towards Bristol docks; a sepia treasure if ever there was one.

This discovery, and my then absolute captivation by all things nautical, led to my Nan telling me about how her father captained the *Cato* between Dublin and Bristol carrying cargoes of Guinness barrels; how Nan would sail with her father during school holidays; and how she then met our grandfather in Bristol et cetera. This was all incredibly exciting and was almost certainly the start of my fascination of the sea, ships, and all things maritime . . .

The *Cato* was one of the first ships to be sunk by a German mine (laid by U29), with only two survivors.

She still lies on the bottom at 51º 23 N 03º 33 W off Nash Point in the Bristol Channel. The barrels of Guinness dispersed up the Channel, landing along the coast at Porthcawl; they were 'rescued' by the locals before marauding Customs officials could confiscate the itinerant rogues. A memorial to *Cato* stands next to the lighthouse in Porthcawl. My daughter took me to visit it after having spent a birthday treat boozy weekend in Dublin celebrating *Cato*. It was a very proud moment.

Footnote: Later in life, I produced a website dedicated to my Great Grandfather and the *Cato*. Built by the Campbelltown Shipbuilding Co, 710 gross tons, speed 10-11 knots, 'The Yacht', known for her sleek lines, would take around five days to make the round trip between Dublin and Bristol.

School & Sea Cadets

I went to school at St James High School in Exeter. Its claim to fame was being penultimate from the bottom of the League Tables for schools in Devon. It was the first year of the Comprehensive system in Devon, and was the boiling pot of two boys' and one girls' secondary school, all mixed together on the site of the old secondary modern girls' school. The two boys' schools had been age-old rivals, with organised fights etc, and the result was chaotic, and at times, pretty damned rough. Bullying was in no short supply and I certainly got my share, often coming home bloodied from the day's beating.

There was a tight-knit group of us 'swats' who had formed a school band. I'm sure that one great magnet for the band members was that of shelter and respite from the incessant mob bullying we suffered. Mr Jennings was at the helm, teaching us to play our instruments, some better than others. Mr Jennings was a terrific guy. He had been a Royal Marine Bandsman and had served on a Destroyer deployed in the Pacific in WWII (from memory, HMS *Repulse* or HMS *Prince of Wales*). His ship had been torpedoed and sunk, with all hands rafted up, many being eaten by sharks. He was one of a couple of hundred survivors out of around 1,500 hands, the rest burning, drowning, or becoming a meal. Mr Jennings was old-school, Victorian even, and a disciplinarian; one did not mess with Mr Jennings.

It was with great sadness that I learnt of his passing away some years later when I was at sea. I'd have loved to have gone to his funeral. There was an advert on the radio years ago about everybody having a memorable teacher who was unforgettable; this always made me think of Mr Jennings. He was a father to me in many ways.

I played E-Flat Bass, moving on to B-Flat Bass, and dabbled with the trombone. At one point, I even attempted the drums! Unfortunately, none of these skills were very transferrable in later life, especially at sea, and I never carried on with them. Years later I did buy an electric guitar, hoping to develop into a clone of my rock star demi-God: my hero, Dave Gilmour. However, not being tenacious, I couldn't be bothered practising and the guitar festered in its case, only to be played by my 'darling daughter' who looked on the internet for twenty minutes, then picked it up and played it. Clearly, she took after her mother, who could play classic guitar, a bit of Flamenco, and the banjo. Not me, who learnt to play knowing which button(s) to press depending where the blob was on the five horizontal lines, and to play a bit longer if the blob was hollow.

PE was boring, and I was disliked by our PE teachers. I hated most conventional sports and couldn't see why the lads loved kicking a bag of wind around a field, or why they got so much attention from girls because they could kick it between three sticks more proficiently than the others.

Cricket seemed bloody stupid: throwing a rock-hard missile towards someone, trying to hit three sticks, while that someone tries to hit it away with a bat. Half the kids would wait around the field just in case the guy with the bat hit the missile near them, in which case they had the dubious honour of having the opportunity to catch said projectile. Fun!

Cross country running was just ridiculous; why would you? Running is bad for your knees and it was done when the weather was crap. Running is a sign of bad planning; leave earlier and walk, or better still, catch a taxi.

The cross-country course consisted of two laps, which passed through some playing fields with a cricket pavilion about halfway around. Simon and I would run the first stage, hide behind the pavilion, smoke a couple of fags, re-join the group on the second lap, and return to the school mid-pack. We would always return mid-pack to ensure we were never picked for a team (we stood out as being slow), or run the risk of having to run a 'third' lap for being lazy.

I enjoyed hockey and throwing the javelin, but trampolining with the girls was always my sport of choice. Simon and I would stand at the base of the trampoline, poised to catch a wayward jumper. Unfortunately, one would have to watch carefully and try not to look up the girls' PE skirts and see their knickers; this was the closest we would get to having sex for a few years to cum.

Irritatingly, it wasn't that I was not a fit, healthy lad. I'd canoed all year-round and cycled miles for fun. I'd canoed, rowed, sailed etc since joining Sea Cadets at fourteen; walked on Dartmoor, and completed Ten Tors: a gruelling 35-mile walk over Dartmoor over two days. I even cycled the eighty miles to Bristol on the Monday after taking our O-Levels, so I was not averse to physical activity; just the conventional games offered to us at school.

At Sea Cadets, we went through a spell of boxing. This sport really is stupid; why would you want to punch a friend, or someone else who didn't pose a threat under normal circumstances? I was rubbish at boxing. I couldn't get myself to hit someone in cold blood and would lose my temper, and all self-control, with anyone that hit me for no proper reason.

I was set up to box with my best mate Dave one evening. We ballet-danced around each other, psyching up for the attacking jab, and then Dave smacked me in the face with his gloved fist. I was totally pissed off. The bastard! I kicked him in the bollocks in retaliation, and that was that; fight over. Obviously, he'd won, but it was him writhing on the deck . . . Whatever.

Academia was of little interest with the exceptions of physics and craft, design, technology. Maths was a bloody difficult hill to climb and subjects like English literature & language, history, and religious education were tedious beyond belief.

In Years 9 and 10 (third and fourth years in those days), geography became of great interest; Suzanne sat beside me just before or after PE, and the sight of her gorgeous legs was way more captivating than barchan dunes or meandering cut-offs. I was infatuated but to have considered asking her out would have been punching way beyond my weight.

My interest in a life on the waves remained undeterred throughout my early years and there was no other career I ever seriously contemplated. I had joined Sea Cadets at fourteen and learnt to sail, row, canoe, ride a bike; all those things you couldn't do before . . . a life of Lil-lets! I wanted to sail with the Queen's Commission but would settle as Bilge Rat if it got me to sea. I had visions of clinging onto the Bridge of a frigate, mid-Atlantic, in a raging storm, firing trajectories at a frightened enemy on the run. I later had images of me clinging onto the poop deck of a Frigate, tweaking intricate parts of the ship's 'whirlybird' against all odds. This image deteriorated into the reality of mooching around a foggy airfield at RNAS Yeovilton or Culdrose; that quickly put paid to any ideas of the Fleet Air Arm! Back to the Bridge for me.

I sat the Royal Navy tests and interviews for an Artificer Apprenticeship in the final year at secondary school. The Physics, Aptitude and Spatial Awareness tests were a breeze; the Mental Arithmetic test was a failure. Sat in terror with two RN interviewers firing questions at me, a Wren barged into the room stating someone had pinched her seat. In true form I retorted that "I would've, but I couldn't reach". I saw my Naval career dissolving into the mist, but one interviewer replied that they needed 'red blood' in the Navy. Hardly PC by today's standards.

Then a great opportunity arose: a day off school to go to a Merchant Navy recruitment day at a hotel in Exeter. No way was I interested in joining a merchant fleet; only the glamour of a fighting machine for me. Then I heard, 'no minimum service, anywhere in the world, own cabin, alcohol, take your wife'. *Woah, I'll have some of that*! I had no thoughts to what a salary meant, but I could still compute that I'd be getting around the world with some freedom, and would have the chance to pack it in if the dream did not manifest itself. And bonking to boot!

Learning French

I am certainly more inclined towards the sciences and find it challenging to speak anything other than English. Like many an ignorant and lazy Brit, I preferred to communicate in English, and just talk more slowly and loudly if the uneducated foreigner couldn't understand me.

At school we had to learn French from day one, and I couldn't wait to give it up in the Third Form when we had to choose our subjects for the forthcoming exams. I just couldn't get interested or understand why on earth anyone would want to learn this wholly academic subject, which would be of no use to anyone in future life; how arrogant and wrong I could be.

At some stage in the Third Form, we were offered the opportunity to go on a French exchange. I had no interest in learning the subject but fancied two weeks away from school, so I begged my parents, duly signed up, and paid (well, more accurately, my parents paid).

I was allocated my exchange partner Jean-Paul; Mrs Love told me carefully that I'd been paired with him because his parents had divorced, and I was from a 'broken home' too. Thanks for that. Divorce in those days was fairly unusual with no Child Support Agency, mandatory maintenance payments, and money being an issue.

Anyway, I'm not sure if my parents were together or apart then, and would need the brain cells of an African elephant to remember this ever-changing detail. My parents' relationship mirrored that of two magnets slowly spinning, suspended alongside each other, alternately attracted and opposed to each other, living together, then parting at spasmodic intervals.

Dave, Nick and I duly bussed off to Rennes to meet our partners, along with the swats who wanted to learn to speak better French and learn about an alternative culture. The three of us were really lucky, as our trio were paired with three lively French lads and a great time was had by all.

We learnt to ride one of the guy's 50cc moped around the school's large car park, something totally unavailable to us in the UK. We all trotted off to the local swimming baths and learnt the parts of the other bathers' bodies, and to swear at each other fluently. We had found a new interest, and the French language had sprung to life, immediately transforming from a dull academic blur to a living thing!

It was from this excursion to the baths onwards that I have loved learning French, and it became one of my top subjects (albeit I horrendously let Mrs Love down by only achieving a B Grade 'O-Level'). This newfound appreciation completely changed my approach to life, and I would use French when ashore as often as possible. On one memorable occasion in '82 I recall using it in Corfu when seeking assistance in a mountain village, having crashed a moped and needing medical help from the non-English speaking locals.

Indeed, I am now married to a French wife, have lived in France, and have several French friends. I would love to have the chance to meet my 'Victorian' French Teacher Mrs Love, and thank her for being such a strict disciplinarian, and enabling me to talk the lingo. Without her, marriage to my French wife would have not been practical.

Musical Taste

Towards the end of school, my musical taste had moved away from Showaddywaddy and Abba, and was elevating to the world of Wishbone Ash and Thin Lizzy. This was almost certainly under the influence of my sister Karen, who was twenty-one months my senior, an eternity at that stage in musical taste. Most of my mates were still into teeny-bob pap but I had a kindred spirit in Nick, with whom I shared a more developed musical taste.

My taste in clothes was changing in parallel to music, and I had started cutting the seams of my trousers up to the knees, and sewing in flower-power material to convert them into flares; scary in retrospect. Similarly, by the Fifth Year, I had rejected standard black uniform shoes and moved into my brown clogs; real hip stuff. My clogs were literally my downfall. I was going out with Margaret, and felt I looked 'the dog's nuts' in my hippy clothes and groovy clogs; that is until I tripped and fell over at her feet. I felt way more at ease in my standard Doc Marten shoes.

Despite this progressive slide into a vaguely more alternative way of expressing myself, I had not yet developed a taste for Pink Floyd, and I recall dinnertimes in the Art Room having to listen to *Dark Side Of The Moon* over and over again, it being the ultimate for fellow classmate Carol, who was the starlet for Mr Hill the Art Teacher. I recall Carol playing the record continuously; monotonous dirge, and wholly depressing.

It is ironic that only a year or two later, the group became my absolute favourite artists of all time, and I now have every album of theirs, including

"Ummagumma" (which I confess is mostly self-indulgent noise).

Plymouth CFE

And there it was. Summer '77 saw me kissing my parents and girlfriend long goodbyes at Exeter St Davids Station. I was leaving my home town to live in Plymouth for two years, training at the Nautical section of the College of Further Education. To be clear, only the kisses with my girlfriend were lingering; otherwise it would have looked odd. The following weekend I came home to see family and imbibe in conjugal rights.

The two years at college was a stretch of my educational attentiveness. I hate studying for the sake of it and the maths lecturer must have been on LSD to be even vaguely interested in the dyslexic world of algebra: differentiation, integration. Really, why would you?

College felt clumsy. It was the height of the punk rock period and us Cadets with our short tidy hair, dressed in black trousers, blazers (with company logos blazoned on the top left pocket), were herded around like sheep. We were ferried between the CFE and residential block like school kids; the Sex Pistols never minding the bollocks and stuff. That said, we were salaried sixteen-year olds, living away from home; a veritable cauldron in which to brew mirth and merriment.

There were circa three hundred navigation (deck) and engineer officer cadets living at the residential building and 'things' were always 'occurring'. The building was ten storeys high, and this led to many a game of launching eggs and other foodstuffs from the windows onto unsuspecting passers-by below. Launching cadets' mattresses down the stairwell was good fun; they just fitted within the surrounds of the handrails, rather like a guillotine.

Motorbikes were banned to First Years by the college. Personally, I had a 1958 BSA C15: a single-cylinder, 250cc slow revving four-stroke; a bang past every lamp post. I had a *provisional* Driving Licence and nothing else.

She was very unreliable, and I had to carry a rucksack full of tools everywhere we went together. The ignition contacts were always slipping, and readjusting the timing was a regular occurrence. I seemed to be continually battling to keep her running and met my match when I sheared the crankshaft. To be fair, I was popping wheelies on the 'old dear'.

I now had to strip down and rebuild the engine, without any college staff knowing of its existence. I removed the engine from the frame, put it in my Adidas holdall, and nonchalantly carried it through the foyer of the residential block to the lifts, and ensconced it into my locker for safe keeping. It was unfortunate that the Head of the CFE Maritime section walked into the foyer as I was mid-flow. Have you ever tried to carry a motorbike engine in a holdall, pretending it is filled with something as light as games kit, and not grimace under the weight? Having got the engine into my locker, I then had to strip the engine down and clean all the parts ready to rebuild. Not so easy without copious amounts of rags.

It just so happened that we changed one sheet and one pillow case per week. We'd line up with the sheet and pillow case neatly folded up until it was our turn to exchange them with 'Matron'. It soon became an obvious solution: on bedding-change days, I would rip the centre square out of the dirty sheet and use this for the repair work. The 'modified' sheet would then be folded up and pillow case put on top, then changed for a new clean ~~rag~~ sheet with which to use that week. I became adept at this, and managed to complete the rebuild with nobody suspecting my rag supplies.

One of my mates, 'Sleebie', enjoyed rock climbing for his hobby. He had all the kit and was dead serious about it. We'd camp at Shaugh Prior on the edge of Dartmoor some weekends, and spend hot sunny days trying to mount Mucky Gully (a high traditional climb in Devon). I was scared of heights and this got the adrenaline pumping.

Having got caught in a 'compromising situation' in Central Park with the college 'bike', I suffered a ban from leaving the residential block (apart from attending college lectures) for several weeks. I obviously had to resort to abseiling out of the sixth-floor window in Sleebie's cabin, out to the real world of clubbing. At the end of the night out, belly full of beers, I'd have to re-scale the outside of the building and climb back through the window of the cabin without being seen.

Matters needed taking in hand, so we stole the key in the break-glass unit by a backdoor fire escape and had over one hundred keys made: one for every Engineer Cadet. The college had very strict rules about the times we were allowed out and this solved all that bureaucratic nonsense. We could now come and go as we pleased. This building is now used by the University of Plymouth, so probably the keys have been returned by Snowflakes.

In the Second Year we all had to do a two-day fire-fighting course at Camels Head Fire Station, Plymouth. This was the usual type of well-controlled training course, all very contrived and safe. We learnt about different extinguishers, how to fight different types of fires, how to use breathing apparatus etc.

Our college had a small contingent of Iranian Cadets who were all around twenty years old, and clever (rich) enough to complete the same course in a second (third or fourth?) language. To us they seemed aloof and didn't mix with us Brits. Looking back, they were older, much more intelligent, from a different class, and abroad.

One assignment was to fight a fire within a compartment using ALBA (air-line breathing apparatus). This was just too much temptation for us. Whilst the Iranian team was in the compartment dutifully trying to extinguish the fire, a British team of Cadets, kitted out with breathing apparatus, carried the air pump into a smoke-filled area, thus pumping thick smoke to the now choking Iranians.

During the course, one Cadet managed to purloin a couple of bags of foam fire extinguisher refill. Mixed under the right conditions with water, an expansion ratio of up to 50:1 was achievable.

Incredibly, following the course, one of the Cadet's girlfriends thought it would be friendly to invite him and his mates to her house party, so about thirty of us went; one bringing the bags of powder. At some point in the evening, the brown powder was mixed and dissolved into the upstairs toilet bowl, whilst the white powder was mixed into the water in the cistern.

One can only imagine the mirth and merriment when an unsuspecting girl had a pee and pulled the flush. Whilst a good proportion of the water was flushed down the loo, a torrent of foam poured out the door, across the landing, down the stairs, and across the reception area.

Later in life (around 2005), recounting this tale to my then neighbour, she was astounded; it turned out that she had been at the party and us geeky Cadets had unknowingly become legends at the college. To that day

I had had no idea we were anything other than "those geeky twats".

I can't say college was all fun and games and I went through serious depression for a while. There was just average shit going on in my life: my family's breakup, I was struggling academically (particularly modern maths), I didn't fit in well with everyone and struggled with self-worth, I'd been dumped by my then serious girlfriend Mary Loose-Knickers (an unfortunate nickname and a misnomer), and it all compounded; a dark cloud above me, and a total sense of 'why bother with life' enveloped me. A cabin mate found me lying on my bunk, plastic bag over my head, tape wrapped tightly around my neck, stemming any flow of breath. I was on the brink. He ran over, tore off the bag and the episode was over. Looking back, it seems odd he kept his promise to me not to tell anyone; nobody else ever knew, or approached me about it. In those days, had the college found out about this incident, this would have ended my career. There was no great understanding of depression back then, and 'psychos' were not appropriate at sea. Depression was to strike again occasionally throughout my life, sometimes instigated by an obvious catalyst, sometimes for no apparent reason.

Being at nautical college, we obviously had to do nautical stuff like swimming, sea survival, how to eat cadavers etc. The deck cadets (navigation officer apprentices) took these lessons very seriously but us "Clankeys" (engineers) certainly did not. Many a time we'd have to do lifeboat drills and there would be a dozen engineer cadets hanging from the ropes, as the lifeboat was lowered off the davits into Plymouth Sound.

Another escapade was when we had to learn how to use distress rockets. These facilitated many opportunities for a laugh. Whilst at the seamanship school one time, it just so happened that the prevailing wind was such that the trajectory, and subsequent parachuting back to Earth of the flare, meant that we could have a competition: who could get the blazing flare to glide casually into the Conoco refinery?

I loved these lessons, poncing around Plymouth Sound playing in boats. I was at home in this playground. The classroom lectures, not so. Being taught much of the theory, and names of the parts of davits, was quite dull. But learning about actual survival techniques was fun: what to eat, drink, and all sorts of trivia. "Water, water everywhere, nor any drop to drink", surviving inches from an unending source of water; the salt makes you thirsty, and can be a killer. Every lifeboat and life raft carry fishing line and hooks but fish should be eaten as a last resort; they are high in protein and the human body needs a lot of water to digest them. There are two main criteria when considering eating your colleagues: one, it is frowned upon (it is best to wait until your meal is dead), and two, we are high in protein and hard to digest without plenty of fresh water.

Whilst learning that the bum and thighs are the places to start with your meal, and cutting them into thin strips and laying the thin slices under the sun to dry was interesting, nothing like this could happen to us; we were young and bad shit only happens to others.

Another thing I pondered on (coming from the South West) was why the 'shite-hawks' didn't eat the neatly prepared homo sapiens' prosciutto laying in the sun to dry? Gulls' stomachs are highly acidic and can digest a car (well, maybe an exaggeration) and if you've eaten fish and chips in Newquay, you'll know they have no table manners.

Don't try this at home. Roll baking powder up in a slice of bread, then throw it into a flock of sea gulls; one less! Hint: keep clear of the 'explosion zone' below.

The college owned a 1928 nineteen-metre Gaff Ketch, *Tectona*. I understand she is now used to offer sailing opportunities to the mentally ill; not a radical change then. We'd go off for a week at a time learning to sail, although most of the Cadets weren't salty seadogs and generally spent the trips hanging over the rails feeding the fish, those on the windward side getting their own back! I sailed as Cook on one such trip, since I was one of the few not busy on the big white telephone. Unfortunately, I could no longer stomach the cooking of meals on the gimbled stove and produced a multi-coloured pancake. So, soup then is it?

Part of our course involved 'sea survival': bobbing around the Channel in an inflated life raft. In the cocoon of a life raft there is no horizon and this leads to horrendous seasickness. This training was planned to take place over two-three days, climbing out of the November waters into the raft, and then freezing one's nuts off together.

We duly sailed on the *Tectona* out of Plymouth Sound into the Channel, then dropped sails to chuck the life raft into the freezing choppy sea. It fell into the chop and half-heartedly semi-inflated into a flaccid blob. The Captain of *Tectona*, an 'Uncle Arthur' bearded seafarer-type, instructed someone to jump into the sea and finish blowing up the blob with the spare air pump.

Not a chance. I ran across the heaving deck, cleared the railings, and landed on top of the raft. I then climbed into the flaccid 'bag', grabbed the air pump, and finished inflating the raft. "Okay, get in the sea now," said Captain Birdseye. My response was in the negative. I stayed predominantly dry throughout my survival experience. Well what is a guy to do?

There are so many tales to tell: Wayne Erasmus rolling his car and writing it off whilst driving down the twisty hill into Looe, Cornwall. To be fair, it was not entirely his fault. He was trying to kill the wasp in the back of the car at the time and the passengers made no move to assist. Another time one guy, having had plaster administered to his leg after coming off his motorbike, asked us to saw his leg plaster so he could bend his knee enough to get back and ride his bike; a quite reasonable request all considered.

It was the Easter Holiday in Year Two when I took my first 'trip'. Myself, my mate Sleebie and his girlfriend 'LB', my mother and my younger sister Cathy, all set off for a week's relaxation on a motor-cruiser on the Norfolk Broads. Mum was separated from Dad (again) and was currently completing her studies at an Occupational Therapy college in Exeter. An odd mixture of folk, but there we go.

One might imagine that two nautical college Cadets would have been thoroughly 'salty' and found this a breeze; wrong! We were engineer apprentices and had not got time for this seamanship nonsense. The 'cruise' entailed a phenomenal amount of drinking and we apparently had a great time.

One particularly eventful day when the others had partaken of a few too many, I was left in control with Cathy, my seven-year-old sister, as ship's mascot. I seem to recall sneakily pouring vast quantities of gin into 'mother', my friends being perfectly capable of doing this themselves (Baileys – yuk!). Anyway, the three of them being soundly unconscious, I took control of the helm and carefully ploughed the boat into the overhanging branches of a rather stout weeping willow. I didn't notice the gouges in the side of the boat, or indeed the smashed windows all along the starboard side.

Cathy and I somehow managed to navigate the boat to Great Yarmouth, where she went to bed and I collapsed. In the middle of the night I was rudely awakened by my somewhat distraught mother shaking me. Apparently, some idiot hadn't registered that the river was tidal.

I had tied the boat up alongside and gone to bed thinking nothing more of it. Unfortunately as the moon crept around the Earth, the water level had descended, rendering the mooring ropes too short and the boat was hanging from the bollards at 45 degrees to the vertical (or was it horizontal? I forget). Having let out plenty of rope, I somehow found my way back to bed where I could curl up and try to contain my thumping headache. I needed to get back to sleep before my hangover truly kicked in.

Mid-morning I was yet again rudely awakened, this time by some 'yellow-welly' boatman who objected to us floating mid-channel. Having let out the mooring ropes, the moon had now fully circumvented the Earth, the water level risen, and the boat was now 'at arm's length' to the bank and was floating around in the 'shipping lanes'.

It was at about this time that the rest of the ship's company emerged and pointed out the damage to the boat. I still blame the tree.

Sleebie and I went off into Great Yarmouth to visit the local glaziers and DIY shops. Having bought filler, paint, panes of glass and putty, we set sail for a quiet lake where we could surreptitiously make amends. We replaced the windows, filled the gouges, painted over all evidence, and prayed we would get our full deposit back.

In those days my salary was around one thousand pounds per annum and we had no spare cash. Mum was a student, a single mother, with a mortgage on top. It was essential that we got our deposit returned or we simply could not have afforded to get home. It was touch-and-go whether my share would buy enough petrol to propel my Honda CB175 to Exeter anyway. In the end I got lost in Hampshire and had the traumatic dilemma of having to decide if I could afford a map. It was a real worry: remain lost or know where I had run out of petrol. The map won and I scraped into Exeter on petrol fumes.

Losing My Virginity

Unlike Richard Branson, losing my cherry was a huge disappointment and I can barely justify a couple of paragraphs to the debacle . . .

At school I had hung around with a very tightly-knit group of friends who were the brunt of much physical bullying by 'the rough kids', and we tended to be fairly 'incestuous' in our partnerships, not venturing out with those outside of our 'academic community', especially not with the 'rough crowd'. Because of this we only really mixed with the 'nice' girls and gained little experience in the sexual department. It is fair to say we were all confirmed virgins with nothing beyond the odd grope to notch up on our headboards.

Progressing to Plymouth CFE, I was aghast to discover that all my classmates had DONE IT, and I was the brunt of much mirth, merriment, and teasing, being the only virgin in the Nautical Department in the college. This was disastrous and I was determined to make amends.

We frequented a pub just next to our digs, the James Street Vaults. This was a pretty dingy affair but it sold alcoholic drinks to all and sundry, and having a baby-face, this was a major plus.

One evening whilst supping ale, a friend pointed out the 'college bike', on which I was guaranteed a ride. All I had to do was to try not to be dumped before I'd done IT. I forget her name but she was a true Muddy Fox: an all-terrain model and good for off-roading apparently. I was all for a bit of bareback!

Having managed to get to a decent party prior to being given the old heave-ho, I duly got her into the back garden, up against the garage. It felt OK, but not quite as

I had previously imagined it; it was not 'in'. This clearly was a position for those of greater (well any) experience, so we gave it a miss and went back to the party, my pride in tatters.

We walked home from the party in the small hours and strolled into Central Park for another go at it. She certainly hadn't been put off by earlier events and we ventured forth to find a nice quiet spot; it being about three am this wasn't difficult. Well, it was OK, but I wasn't really sure what all the fuss was about.

When I divulged my news the following day, whilst on the bus to college, I was a little surprised that almost all of my mates were dead keen to know what it was like; each one now admitting to being a virgin! What a plank. I'd taken their bait hook, line, and sinker; they'd all blagged about their past.

Obviously the 'relationship' frittered to an abrupt halt. I don't remember ever talking to her again, mission having been accomplished, and me clearly not being to her requisite standard. I didn't care. I'd DONE IT!!!

The price of doing it was higher than expected (even though I hadn't actually paid). Word got out about my escapades of the soiree and I was duly grounded by the college for several weeks. But that was nothing; she'd given me NSU.

The moral of the story is: "If you must play with bikes, stick to motorbikes" (and make sure they're not clapped out).

Sheep Digging

During the winter of '78 there was a heavy dumping of snow across the country and the South West got more than its annual dose. Dartmoor was badly hit and the farmers suffered, but not as badly as the sheep, who became buried under several feet. Stupid buggers could've moved as the snow fell, no?

Dartmoor's natural beauty was surpassed yet again, the snow-white duvet covering the normally green quilt of heather and gorse. The grey skies, heavy with snow, sat atop the white landscape, the Tors looking like giant stalagmites covered in icing sugar.

A number of us Cadets were training for the Ten Tors expedition to be held in '79 and regularly went yomping on the moors, training for the big day. We were asked by one of our lecturers to go help farmers dig out buried sheep, so off we went, crowded in the college Land Rover, followed by a few of the guys' cars. Wayne, one of our Welsh mates, seemed particularly excited and expectant. Maybe he'd over-estimated just how grateful those sheep would be? Or maybe just because they were trapped.

We spent the morning digging and celebrating the release of the daft buggers; good fun but exhausting. In the afternoon we felt a little relaxation was in order, so we got plastic sacks and the like to use as toboggans. One Cadet with part-Norwegian parentage just happened to have a pair of skis (as one did in those days). We took it in turns to plant ourselves face-first into the wet English snow, plastic skis strapped to our feet, unable to get up from this prostrate position, at the mercy of the other guys; and Wayne.

Having spent an hour or two like this, we decided to 'Go Large'. Being engineering apprentices, it didn't take too long to remove the bonnet from one of the cars and use it as a surrogate sledge. This proved awesome fun and well worth the resultant damage to the bonnet. The bonnet proved such a good sledge that the river at the bottom of the field became the next problem to overcome. I don't recall ever finding a solution to the river problem, but most of us ended up soaking wet and freezing cold, the bonnet being left at the farm for disposal. A scrap yard close to the college provided the answer to replacing the crumpled bonnet.

Later the following year when we had finished our exams, were due to be disbanded and venture off to sea, it was necessary to rid ourselves of our cars, which were unfit for transport by the majority of Humankind (or otherwise). The college car park provided the answer, and hours of fun.

Apart from a few, the majority of the cars were in dire need of TLC, and many not really retrievable in terms of bodywork or MOTs. The Church of Scientology building's gable-end made up one end of the car park and this became the centre of our entertainment, driving the cars as fast as we dared into the wall, head on, glancing blows, anything to destruct the vehicles. This was great fun, even for those of us who hadn't actually learnt to drive at that juncture.

Years later, I blagged a letter to the DVLA begging to take my driving test before the end of my leave and going back to sea. My date came through: two weeks' time. At that stage, driving friends' cars into walls and doing handbrake turns (allegedly) was the full extent of my driving experience. It's fair to say I took 'another' crash course. I passed within the two weeks having had seventeen lessons. I was an appalling driver but legal.

MV British Commodore

Finally, we all escaped the college and set off for two three-month trips back-to-back. I received my orders to join my first ship; surely, I'd really pissed off someone at the British Tanker Company Ltd? The MV *British Commodore*, a sixty-nine thousand-ton crude oil tanker, renowned in the Company as an unreliable piece of junk, was my first mission. Built in Govan in 1967, she was past her best and had a reputation of being bloody hard work. Joining with a college mate, Taff (Welsh just in case you weren't sure) and another Cadet, we stepped off the air-conditioned aeroplane after the seven-hour flight, and bashed our noses on the forty degrees centigrade wall of ambient atmosphere at Dubai airport. Oh my God, and this was just the evening!

We dutifully waited in the Astoria Hotel in Dubai for a week, eating our way through a month's salary of meals, whilst the *Commodore* lumbered from breakdown to breakdown, finally finding its way to the Gulf. Eventually, a minibus arrived to whisk us off across the desert to Ras-Al-Khaimah (then a tiny village of a few huts and a rickety pontoon) where the pilot launch awaited us. Finally, we were being 'launched' into our sea-faring careers. We jumped from the deck of the launch onto the pilot's ladder as the launch rose and fell on the heavy swell, then inadeptly climbed up the rope ladder onto the main deck.

We had dropped the title of Cadet and risen to the dizzy heights of being called 'Apprenti' (apprentices?).

The first morning, the necessity for copious amounts of drinking water, and the intake of numerous salt tablets, was drilled into us by our fellow officers. Being totally green at this stage, we digested the requirement to thoroughly chew before swallowing the enteric-coated salt tablets. This we did whilst gorging on FEB (full English breakfast). Unfortunately, we had made our first mistake in not considering that the more experienced officers had duped us, as we ran to jettison our stomach contents over the side.

We descended into the engine room to meet the engineers and get our first taste of a ship's heart. The main engine was something to behold. A two-stroke, six-cylinder, eighteen-thousand bhp Burmeister & Wain diesel engine. To see and experience an engine of this size for the first time is incredible. Each cylinder has its own individual cylinder head of about eight-foot diameter, with six eighteen-inch exhaust valves, each in their own cage, all with an open rocker assembly (approximately six foot across), and runs between nineteen and ninety-six rpm.

The ship was manoeuvring at Dead Slow Ahead whilst picking up stores etc and the engine was ticking over at around twenty rpm. What the Fuck, how can a combustion engine continue running and not stall at this pace? Eventually stores were loaded, and the revs slowly increased until we were going Full Ahead at ninety-six rpm. Whoopee doo! The rockers now looked like a row of guys with a dose of crabs doing semaphore, or a very stilted Mexican wave.

The temperature was mid-forties, it was very humid and extremely noisy; a massive culture shock to us. But we were really fortunate to have joined at that time and were given an interesting first project. One of the reciprocating air compressors had failed. We were instructed to strip it down, then report back to the Second Engineer. This we did with gusto, decapitating its limbs with gay abandon: a race to disgorge this helpless six-legged monster.

Rendered helpless and naked to its core, we dutifully reported back to 2E, who felt it extremely amusing that we should not have noticed that the compressor was not in fact connected to any pipework and had not been in use for years. Having totally embarrassed us with our lack of intuition and common sense, he struck the final blow: "Rebuild it." Now here's the thing, if three of you race to get a machine into pieces and nobody takes note of how you've achieved this, you need to call the AA (Automobile Association, not Alcoholics Anonymous). This lesson has stayed with me for life, as has the Chief Engineer's saying: "An engineer never panics, he merely shows concern." To this day I have always strived to live by these two lessons, not always successfully, but I am trying.

Our OND results came out whilst away at sea and I was astounded to have passed maths, albeit I scraped through with minimum percentage marks. To pass the OND it was necessary to pass a set number of subjects, but maths was compulsory. Maths was a prolonged struggle for me and passing was no mean feat.

I was celebrating with great gusto in the officers' bar following the news and was well into a bottle of Bacardi (or two). I was perched on a bar stool, chatting to the Chief Engineer (not a common occurrence) who didn't take kindly to me at the best of times. At some point I fell unconscious, tumbling backwards off the bar stool, cracking my head on the low table behind me.

A life-long message I had learnt from the Chief was that of speaking the truth. I was very wary of him and tied myself in knots over a very simple issue, which

I had compounded in lies. Had I owned up at the start, all would have been well in the world.

A log is taken every four hours (and entered into the engineering logbook) when watchkeeping, and all the machinery parameters are recorded at the end of each watch, in order for comparison, and to see any untoward changes. Of course, tank dip readings will change with the ship's position in the water and if the volume in a given tank doesn't change over the period, the dip reading will change as the ship rises or lowers in or out of the sea as the ship's cargo is loaded or discharged.

We were discharging our cargo, and towards the end of the watch, it was my duty to 'do the log'. I went from place to place, noting and recording the myriad of temperatures, pressures and depths etc. Time was short, the engine room hot, and I was keen to get 'up top', and ashore. Stupidly, I didn't bother to take the sounding of the main engine sump; it had been the same for weeks.

Unfortunately, in my naivety, I hadn't considered that the ship's bows were rising out of the water as we discharged our cargo, and that the cargo tanks emptied by the hour; hence the sounding changed (even though the content remained the same).

The Chief Engineer picked up on this when he checked the log, and he was on the warpath, demanding where we had 'lost' the oil. This was my time to put my hand up and admit my erroneous ways. No, too dangerous. I remained adamant that I had dipped the tank and that my reading was correct. We spent an hour or more searching the bilges for the 'lost' oil, despite it being painfully obvious that I had 'flogged the log'.

I dug my hole deeper and deeper. The more I dug, the more I couldn't back out and come clean. I created havoc for all, and extended engine room time for my colleagues, hot and bothered, mindlessly searching on a fool's errand.

The Chief surely knew the truth, as did my colleagues, and the lie got worse; I was too afraid to admit the initial lie.

When I had to go for my end-of-trip report from the Chief, he had been very fair in my assessment, but stated that: "Between you and me, you have a drink problem". I retorted: "Yes Chief, you banned me from the bar". I'm not sure I had grasped the gravity of his statement.

We had to carry out certain major tasks during our early trips and record them in our 'training log book'; the Chief or Second Engineers then signed them off as completed. At the end of the trip I added a few tasks in addition to the standard ones but forgot to get them signed off, so I forged the Chief's signature. I had done the tasks, and the records were correct, but I'd still forged the signature.

This caught up with me in a later trip, when the same Chief joined as relieving-Chief, and saw my log book with 'his' signatures. This episode saw me dragged up to BP's Head Office Britannic House (Big Panic House as it was fondly known) for a disciplinary hearing with HR (Human Remains). I squirmed and wriggled and pleaded for my career. Fortunately, I was able to convince BP to continue with my employment, and my career was saved.

Even better still, although my parents asked to read my letter from Head Office, I was able to blag my way out of this corner and they never found out about my verbal disciplinary.

Mombasa

First stop: Mombasa. Five days trying to discharge our cargo whilst the lumbering pumps kept 'falling over'. Now I obviously don't know what you know about Mombasa, but for an eighteen-year-old lad, it was Heaven. We'd heard all of the 'Uncle Albert seadog' stories about hedonistic runs ashore, but this was indescribable. Mombasa was a great place to go: loads to do and see, bars aplenty, great beer, fun nightclubs and scores of 'loose' women.

Prior to going to sea we'd all heard about the outrageous adventures others had seen and experienced, and it was with scepticism that we ventured ashore, not believing the exaggerated yarns of older students at college, who had already had a taste of a life on the ocean waves. Thus, Mombasa came as somewhat of a surprise. From Plymouth CFE we had graduated to the West African town which can only be described as nigh-on hedonistic.

The town was entered by passing under a pair of enormous concrete tusks, and consisted of shanty huts surrounding shady nightclubs, the whole place littered with beggars, bros and whores. I felt tense with the excitement of being in a foreign land, surrounded by such seedy characters; the unknown, potential danger lurking everywhere, and the physical suspense of being so far from the steady reality of home.

Having passed under the tusks, it was like an African 'Wonderland', only there were 'Alices' all around us, costing only five pounds per night. It felt like we'd died and gone to Heaven. A group of us ventured into a night club on the first night and my eyes nearly popped out of my head. We were pounced on by the most beautiful women, all seeming intent on one thing, which fortunately coincided with our ideas. We drank and danced and selected our partners. We learnt how it was bad form to be a 'butterfly' and flit from one woman to another each night. What an odd concept, being faithful to a 'Sweet Painted Lady'.

Nightclub was a cute term which vaguely described what was clearly a 'knocking-shop'. A small dance floor was mostly full of couples who clearly could not be bothered getting a room, or cared who was watching. The goings-on were well beyond anything within my experience; certainly a world apart from the clubs in Exeter.

Tusker was the local brew and we did our best to assist with the brewery's monthly profit. It was a really palatable beer. Not many countries could satisfy my taste buds, with me being then an active member of CAMRA (Campaign for Real Ale). Having had a skin-full, we each ventured off on our separate ways and learnt the ways of life many times over.

My partner for the séjour was a Miss Doris K. Call me a sceptic, but I'm not wholly convinced that was her real name. We passed a very pleasurable five days and I was captivated by her cultural stories, such as the time she nearly stepped on a cobra whilst hanging out the washing. She was bloody gorgeous (until she took off her wig). She had a Brillo pad down her nether regions, or so it seemed.

Mombasa was my first ever run ashore and was a culture shock in many ways. It was my introduction to real poverty and professional begging. This was London begging, genetically modified: amputees who had had limbs removed by their parents to make them more appealing to the more charitable visitors. On several occasions I gave the majority of my shore-money away and it was difficult to toughen-up to the harder side of life.

Times were tough there, money was scarce and mugging was an ever-present threat, although I never actually tried it. After a night out, we'd stagger back to the ship for the day's work. I don't recall ever feeling any fear of being mugged, or ending up dead behind a tin hut; just bewildered at this crazy period of our lives, so far from the reality of Blighty.

Mombasa is a popular holiday resort, and I wonder how punters feel about the poverty and debauchery there whilst browsing, pockets bulging with money to burn?

Back on the *Commodore,* the boiler was high pressure, and the feed water was prone to acidity due to the water being made from sea water by the evaporators. It was necessary to test for Ph daily, administering an alkali to the boiler to ensure neutrality. This particular ship, the chemical used was a powder called CTC, which was very caustic and dangerous. It was critical to add the required dose of CTC to a pre-filled two-gallon bucket of warm pure water. The engineer concerned decided to take a short cut, by pouring the water onto the powder chemical, which he had measured into the empty bucket. Ever tried adding baking powder to an eggcup of vinegar? Or used a foam extinguisher? Ever mixed weed killer and sugar? Don't - an old schoolmate of mine lost his thumb doing this.

Anyway, we heard the engineer's screams from around the engine room, and bundled him under a fire hydrant. I'm not sure he fully appreciated the salt water poured over his skinless face and body, but nobody had COSHH data sheets to hand; in fact, COSHH meant

'Truncheon' in those days. He was allowed a week off to recover, and returned on watch five days later looking like an Egyptian Mummy, straight out a comic book.

Safari

Whilst in port in Mombasa, it became necessary to 'pull' a main engine piston. Now these are circa ninety-six cm bore and one-point-six-metre stroke, so a piston and piston rod are some four-five metres long weighing in at several tons. Each cylinder head nut was handi-matic, being removed with a five-foot, inch-thick spanner and a fourteen-pound sledge hammer. The Second Engineer gave the three Engineer Cadets a choice: help with this heavy operation, or go on a long day's safari for the princely sum of twenty-five pounds. After a nano-second's profound consideration, we unanimously agreed that on balance, maybe the safari might just prove the favourable option. Forty-degrees Centigrade, eighty percent plus humidity, and bloody hard graft didn't hold the same appeal somehow.

We set off in a mini-van very early the next morning; apprentices, a few off-watch officers and a couple of wives. The morning African sun pulled itself up and over the horizon as we bounced along in the jalopy, heading further from civilization, towards the savanna.

The safari was amazing; we saw all the usual suspects roaming the plains and went off-piste chasing a pride of lions, interrupting their daily hunt. With the open-top roof I guess it's just as well we kept the four wheels firmly planted on terra firma. Herds of elephants, giraffe, zebra, and any number of flashy antelope kept us amused for hours. The scenery was one long shoot from David Attenborough's *Planet Earth;* we were all appropriately blown away, feeling privileged to share this with nature. My Kodak Instamatic quickly chewed its way through the reel of 100 ASA film.

'Safari-ing' is thirsty work and the 'beer fairy' called. Stopping at a quiet spot, we stood under a thatched umbrella sipping a few well-earned cold Tusker, looking around at the surrounding spectacle. "Look out for that big spider above your head", called out a shipmate. Now, I'd been caught out before by the more experienced officers, and I'm not stupid. "Yeah, yeah, yeah", was my response. Eventually, persuaded to glance skywards, a fist-sized hairy monster was dangling from its rope. Cross-country running suddenly became my preferred sport.

After a hard day's shooting, we put our cameras away and headed back to port, the married guys and gals back to the ship, whilst the younger ones amongst us headed for more engaging activities with the locals. What a way to round off the day.

Jungle Village

Taff and I decided to explore up the river whilst at Mombasa, so we set off with several packs of cigarettes and as many beers as we could get in our haversacks. Through the port we walked, trying not to get 'jumped' by the dodgy-looking dock-workers, until we hit a dead stop at the port fence.

Not to be deterred, we climbed over the fence, fingers-crossed the armed guards didn't spot us. Having successfully scaled the first obstacle, we ventured on upriver into the jungle. I can't pretend we weren't naive and shit-scared.

Our fear reached a crescendo as we ambled accidentally into a real jungle village, mud huts with straw roofs and all. A swarm of kids surrounded us, begging for something or other; adults looking up but not moving towards us, we looked around for the cauldrons in which we would surely be cooked for dinner. What seemed odd was that the locals were obviously leading a very primitive lifestyle, but all wore denim cut-off jeans and sported various T-shirts: "I'm just popping to Marks & Spencer, Dear."

In true British style we emptied our haversacks and dished out our fags and cans of booze. These were met with polite 'thank yous' (or something that sounded grateful) and smiles. We sat and drank with them and drew on our cheap ship's cigarettes (we didn't think that we were affecting their health at the time).

The kids then taught us how to climb palm trees, and we all swam in the river together having a great laugh, not understanding a word the other was saying. It was a very special day and I hold it dear in my memory. I was from Exeter in Devon, where there was no prejudice (in those days) and I cherish the feeling of our different colours and backgrounds being transcended by the most basic of things: fags 'n' booze. It's such a shame the world isn't like this today.

Taff and I finally had to make a move back to the *Commodore*, so we said our goodbyes and walked off back down the river, having tasted just a morsel of other people's lives.

Back at the ship, the Indian crew were proudly showing off a number of deadly poisonous snakes they'd caught whilst fishing in the same river we had swum in earlier.

Nurses Party

Melbourne was a great place to go. The other side of the world, and it wouldn't have passed my mind as possible a few years beforehand. Australia was very clean and organised, people were polite, courteous, and followed rules: odd for a country of convicts' offspring.

In the bars, beer was sold to customers in jugs, but with small 'whisky glasses' to drink from, it being polite to top up the glasses from the jug, and drink with decorum. Well, this got boring, so we ordered a jug each and drank from them. It was with surprise that we were asked to leave a bar in Australia for being uncouth. We later also got ejected from a local massage parlour. Apparently, Ozzy massage parlours only offer massages, not like other ports around the world.

I phoned home from a land-based phone. We had probably only recently had a telephone installed at home, and I knew Mum would be surprised and thrilled to hear from me. I forgot the time difference. Communication has moved on so far in the interim. I would talk, then wait several seconds for Mum to hear my voice over the waves, then she'd reply. A few seconds later I'd hear her reply and respond. A conversation took ages and that's without mis-hearing or mis-understanding each other. At that time, we had a party-line with our next-door neighbour. To those below 'a certain age', this meant the two houses shared a telephone line; if you picked up the receiver to make a call and heard chatting, your neighbour was on the phone and you had to hang up and wait.

Customs officials could be fun and interesting, or horrendously officious. We kept two bottles of whisky behind the bar, one for guzzling, and one with a little bit of pee in it; this we offered freely to any Customs official that gave us a hard time. The poor unsuspecting soul in Melbourne fitted that mould. Not only did we ply him with 'Urinefiddich' but I asked him to show us his convict number tattooed on his arm. It's fair to say that he left with his tail between his legs.

Later in life I returned to Oz for an extended family holiday; it was great, but unrecognisable as the country of the early Eighties.

The *Commodore* was sat ('sat' is an odd term; we were floating) at a jetty on the coast of Melbourne and we had invited the nurses at the local hospital to a party we'd arranged for them in our officers' bar. The take-up was good. As apprentices, there was little chance of an getting a sniff (so to speak), so we stuck to drinking in excess.

A great time was had by all, especially the more senior officers. One officers' family lived near Melbourne, and they came onboard to visit him and enjoy the party. They brought their teenage daughter with them, but she seemed less than impressed with the proceedings, so I offered to show her the engine room. I found this place fascinating, so why wouldn't she? It was suggested in the bar that I might show her the 'golden rivet', which gave way too much banter and merriment. We left the bar, me trying to look knowledgeable and wondering what the hell a 'golden rivet' was; bless. It's fair to say we never found a golden rivet, and that her fascination for marine engineering didn't equal mine.

Copious amounts of cheap beer were clearly going to be the order of the day and I recall laying down, barely conscious, on the bar floor in the early hours; the married guys and the lucky few having disappeared to their cabins long ago.

Now I don't wish to be sexist or offensive, but lying next to me was a woman who may have been half-decent looking prior to the bus running into her.

I think I nearly turned to religion that night. I had lain there for a good few minutes, thinking whether I could or couldn't; but possibly God delivered me from all evil. I fell unconscious and clearly didn't.

Fishing

The *Commodore* was barely able to scrape her carcass into Mombasa port on a spring high tide, so when we returned for our second stint after the Australian tour, we were destined to drift near the river mouth for a couple of days.

Hanging over the stern was suspended a forty-five-gallon oil drum with both ends opened; this acted as a wind shield for dropping our detritus into the 'pond'. After drifting around for a day or two, fifteen-foot-plus 'Nobby Clarks' homed in on our ship, circling the stern with great interest. These were amazing to us young lads, who'd never seen anything beyond a five-foot blue shark strung up in Looe, Cornwall!

Obviously, the order of the day was to catch and eat these white-tipped reef monster man-eaters, but meat hooks (for hanging bovine carcasses in the freezer) merely bent and gave way to the wrench of a severely pissed off one-tonne dinosaur. Out of frustration, I ventured into the engine room and made a particularly unforgiving hook out of inch-steel bar, looped onto a metre-long inch-steel wire strop. The strop, then being attached to one of the ship's mooring ropes, wound around the port-side steam-driven winch. The two aft winch drums were circa five-foot diameter, driven by twin steam reciprocating eight-inch pistons; pretty damned powerful things all told.

Having purloined large lumps of cow from the galley, we fixed these to the leviathan hook, released the winch brake and lobbed it over the 'wall' into the pond. With the thrash of a tail, the meat, hook and Nobby disappeared into the distance, with the winch drum accelerating from standstill to fifty rpm in the blink of an eye. Allowing the fish to play out a few hundred feet, the brake was slowly applied, and the missile contained. We then played the shark, winding it in close to the ship, then letting it shoot off into the abyss. Having tired the shark (and bored of the fun under the sweltering sun), it became apparent we then needed to somehow get this monster onto the Poop Deck. As luck would have it, and with an engineer apprentice's cunning, we resorted to passing the buck. Now this may seem just a tad un-PC by today's standards, but the *Commodore's* crew were an Indian gang who weren't allowed alcohol; who were we not to take advantage of this fact?

Having managed to tire the shark, now knackered and drifting at the ship's stern, for the princely sum of a case of beer (stolen from the officers' bar), we bribed a number of Indians to descend to sea level in a lifeboat and secure the second mooring rope around the shark's tail. Unsurprisingly, this didn't fit the shark's plans, and was quite a spectacle for us lads peering over the poop deck rails.

Having finally secured the non-toothed end of the shark to the mooring rope, the crew motored their lifeboat hell-for-leather back to the hooks of the lifeboat davits, trying to avoid the wrath of Nobby's jaws. Once back on board, us apprentices stood bravely watching on the next deck up, whilst the Indian crew members winched the hapless beast onto the poop deck, adjacent the winches. It must have been a day or two before we decided the shark must be dead, and approach close enough to cut into bite-size chunks and remove the trophy jaw.

Fishing was a great sport for us bored lads. No namby-pamby trout or pike for us; catfish and remora were our preferred prey. In our spare time, under a blazing sun, in sandals and cut-off jeans, we'd while away many an hour catching these fish with untold makeshift lines, hooks and bait. Catfish were always great fun when deck and engineer apprentices fished together. Invariably, it would turn into a fight between the two factions, each hurling catfish at the other, and trying to get the barbs stuck into each other's backs. Remora offered similar entertainment, trying to get the high-suction sticker onto the opposition's backs, only to be cut off with deck knives. Generally, it would be the fish that was cut off, rather than the other's torso.

All of the fleet's ships had sea water swimming pools, filled in warmer climes from the fire main. Now I wasn't on this particular ship, but I have heard this 'Kentucky Fried Mouse' story sufficient times to believe its roots. Allegedly, after a few drinks and a day's fishing, it was felt it would be quite amusing to catch a smaller (presumably five or six-foot) shark and set him free in the ship's swimming pool. This was probably a good laugh until the poor officers coming off the twelve-to-four watch, having ensconced several cans of Export, decided to cool off for a swim before breakfast. I guess the dorsal fin stopped them from being breakfast.

Eventually the fun had to come to an end and we set sail for Australia, a five-day hike across the Pacific. This was a long-haul, and the seas provided a beautiful swell, but not enough to upset our stomachs.

We watched dolphins playing in our bow wave, the dolphins showing off their prowess, leaping skyward, and plunging back into the deep, and a few whales off the ship's sides, following our movement through the seas.

Leaning over the ship's side watching the bows carve their way through the deep blue sea was mesmerizing, and I had spent hours leaning over the 'wall', watching the spume ejected off the ship as she ploughed her way through the Pacific. The skies were blue and the sea bluer. It was warm and it felt fantastic: the freedom, the power of the sea, and Nature in its full glory.

Our officers' bar was for'd facing across the main deck and on to the horizon.

It made absolute sense for the duty navigation officer to spend the evening in the officers' bar having a quiet drink, occasionally glancing to the horizon, whilst the crewman on the Bridge did the serious watch-keeping.

Sailing back up from Oz on the return trip to the Gulf, we had acquired an albatross, which sat gliding without so much as a twitch of its wings, following us for over a week. The genetically-modified 'shite-hawk' seemed to hang motionless, like a kid's mobile, never moving from its position just off our poop deck. One morning, it had presumably got bored or lonely and had turned tail for home.

Albatrosses (albatri?) are the most elegant birds imaginable: huge wingspan as they glide, suspended on the breeze, never need to flap their wings; really cool budgies are albatri.

SS British Reliance

The *Commodore*, like many in the fleet, had been a work-hard, play-hard ship, and great fun. This was a huge contrast to our second ship the SS *British Reliance*, which we joined with no leave between the two trips. She was a two hundred and seventy-eight thousand-ton VLCC (very large crude carrier, or super tanker to landlubbers). This ship was tramping around Europe and was manned by 'steam-queens' and a few of their wives.

The *Reliance* (later used in the making of *Superman III*) was staggeringly unremarkable. The modus operandi was serious conversation and extremely dull leisure after the fun of an old motor ship. We tramped around North West Europe and not much to retell.

Having visited such far-off and exotic parts on the *Commodore*, I was extremely disappointed to learn I was to join my second ship in Wilhelmshaven, on the north coast of Germany. We'd been to Dubai, Kenya, Adelaide, Melbourne and all manner of other exciting places, and had even been on a real safari to see a wide selection of wild African beasts.

The *Commodore* had been much older than the Reliance and *her* accommodation was 'tired'. Taff and I had shared a two-berth cabin with bunk beds, the 'heads' being shared with other apprentices, remote and several yards down the corridor. My cabin on the *Reliance* was about twenty feet plus in both directions and I had my own ensuite toilet and shower.

I woke the first morning thinking that it was odd that we didn't seem to have left port; we'd been scheduled to sail overnight. I looked out my cabin window to discover land was nowhere to be seen, having disappeared during the twilight hours. It was odd that I hadn't been woken by the engine's noises or vibrations.

The *Commodore's* colossal diesel engine was started by ten-Bar compressed air, injected into each cylinder in firing order via a distributor, the air forcing each piston down and the engine turning a revolution or two, until the air was shut off and fuel injected. The resultant melody was a large *TTTTSSSSH, WHUUUUMP, WHUUMP, whuump*, followed by the drumming of the engine; all being heard from the bar, cabins, and all over the accommodation. This was the reassuring sound of the engine starting, and no necessity for the engineers to dive down to the engine room to rescue the watchkeepers in the event of no-start.

The *Reliance*, being driven by a steam fan, would start slowly and build up to Dead Slow Ahead over a few seconds, gracefully and with decorum. The result of this was that the watchkeepers were privy to a *shhhHHHhhh* as the main steam inlet valve gently introduced the sixty-Bar medium to the turbine blading, and the accommodation occupants would be unaware of the manoeuvre, unless their ear was placed on the deck, spying audibly on the beast below.

A tanker's propeller would generally be four or five-bladed, up to a fifty-foot phosphor bronze monstrosity, which did not care to slip or cavitate, unlike smaller, faster-revving propellers, and they would take umbrage at being turned when the ship was not moving through the water. In fact, once the ship was moving beyond slow speed manoeuvring, the hull would move through the water at the speed of the pitch of the propeller at each revolution: i.e. like a screw in a piece of wood. From stopped, this was not possible and the propeller would not be able to move the ship by its pitch, resulting in the ship's stern jumping around as though it had a dose of crabs, especially on the smaller 'River Boats'. The more sedate start of the steam-ship's turbine also had the secondary effect of the stern not being thrashed about, which made the manoeuvring more comfortable for the ship's complement: allowing the hulk to slip her moorings undetected by the sleeping.

This was my first trip with a 'white' crew and there were some remarkable differences. There was a gay Second Cook on board, and whilst we used the term 'bummer' and other such non-discriminatory terminology at school, we were naive, and I don't think I really knew what it meant, the word's implications, or that there really were guys who preferred same-sex relationships.

Some ships had the ability to sail 'UMS' (unmanned machinery space). This entailed the engineers to work 'normal working hours' Monday to Friday, carrying out general maintenance and repairs, and Saturday mornings when we would carry out specific planned maintenance routines. One engineer would be the duty engineer for twenty-four hours, and it would be their role to manage the operations of all ship's machinery, and general watchkeeping.

Electricity at sea was generated at 440 volts and 60 hertz for economy reasons. This wouldn't affect most appliances, but it did some. These were the heady days of tape recordings; probably preceding CDs by a decade. I had what was then a trendy Sony Walkman, a mobile tape player one could carry around with a strap around the shoulders. There's a hunk on the front cover demonstrating said article. These machines would occasionally to chew and spit out the tape from the cassette, creating a cat's cradle, and destroying the tape.

If one was very lucky it was possible to wind the tape back into the cassette without twisting it. Our music would be played on said tape recorders; which had synchronous motors i.e. they ran at a set speed directly proportional to the supply frequency. These were designed around the 50 hertz supplies ashore; not the 60 hertz aboard ships; hence all music was played exactly 20% faster than intended. The good news is that the incessant *Eagles* and *Neil Diamond* played by the more senior officers in the bar was over-with more quickly. The downside of this is that they could play the same bloody tape more times per hour.

When running UMS it was the engineer apprentice's job to collect the lunches for all of the engineers from the galley and carry them down to the engine room's control room. This involved negotiating stairways and vertical ladders, whilst on a rolling deck and carrying the food trays. The trays themselves were an art form. They consisted of multiple layers of trays (the same we had used at school), held apart from each other by a stud bar with locking nuts. This could be really tricky, balancing on a rolling ship, climbing down ladders, afraid to spill someone's lunch and have to repeat the process.

I think the only occurrence of any memorable value from that trip was one of my forays to the galley in quest for our food. It was a lumpy sea and the ship was rolling heavily. I had to have a four-tier tray topped up with a random selection of food and get it back across the obstacle course to the hungry engineers. Having got the tray arrangement half loaded, the ship lurched and a few plates slid off the trays and smashed on the stone-tiled deck. The Second Cook (gay, unbeknown to me) dived towards me, bending down to pick up the pieces.

In my infinite naivety, thinking I was being funny, I asked him to, "do me a favour while you're down there." This was the last time I did this without a little forethought, but it did offer much merriment to the other galley staff!

Glasgow College

Having had a couple of weeks leave over Christmas '79 following the trip on the *British Reliance*, I was due to go back to college the first week of January '80 to complete the OND Supplementary Certificate. I had been allocated Glasgow for this course and imagined twelve months of living in hell, coming back to England with a Heidelberg scar and other bottle-neck injuries.

I sold my Honda CB175 and dashed out to buy my beloved Suzuki GS750, on which I would load up and move to Scotland for the year. On arrival one evening in the darkness, I stopped to ask directions to the college from a Glaswegian local. The college would accommodate us for three nights, by which time we'd have to move out into our own digs. The college was just on the edge of the Gorbals on the banks of the Clyde and the accent was strong. Not having understood a word of the directions offered to me, I'd ride around the corner and repeat the process. Did they speak a foreign language up here, Jimmy?

Glasgow College was very different to Plymouth CFE. The lessons were academic, but applied. Instead of trying to compute the algebraical hieroglyphics that the Plymothian maths lecturer had tried to imprint on our brains, now we'd calculate beam or shaft strengths, design ship sections etc. Rather than having had to learn a heap of seemingly ungainly mathematical equations around electrical transformer losses and the like, we'd learn about star-delta starters and other practical applications, making things far more interesting for all.

Living in digs, away from home, and out of the clutches of the college staff was amazing; and costly. I was fanatical about motorcycling and rode my 'Suzi' all over Scotland (and to Devon for the holidays - a nine hundred-mile return trip). The throttle was digital control in those days: On or Off. I did my bit to decrease the ozone layer, although we'd no idea about such things back then.

Drink and drugs consumed much of the remainder of my spare cash, having paid out for rent and petrol; food was an unnecessary expense. My mother and younger sister came up to visit me in the summer holidays and Mum burst into tears at the train station when met by her pony-tailed, ear-ringed Biafran, in a cut-off Afghan coat, jeans and sandals. It's fair to say I had turned a little 'hippy-ish'.

In the second half of the year I succumbed to malnutrition and was too ill to get to college for several weeks. I was then living on potatoes (whole mashed potatoes on their own) at the Doctor's insistence, too ill to get out of bed for some time. I lay in bed reading James Herbert's *The Rats*, whilst our flat's mice would scurry around looking for our leftovers and other rubbish.

Glasgow was a great place to be a student. England still had strict laws over pub opening hours, whereas Glasgow's entire economy revolved around alcohol consumption twenty-four hours a day, it seemed.

Despite the reputation Glasgow had in those days it was a great city with lovely people. Sure, being English you were met with derision from all, but it wasn't personal, and the veneer melted into warmth and friendliness when one-to-one with the Scots. I lived just off Biers Road (a famous student area) and used to hang out with a bunch of guys with motorbikes. One of the guys used to build 'hogs' for the Hells Angels, and had a thick, raw Glaswegian accent. He was very hard to understand at best and hated the English with a vengeance; except he didn't, and was a real hoot once plied with McEwan's. We'd zoom off into the Trossachs or head south to Ardrossan on sunny days.

On many a weekend we'd down a few McEwan's, load up someone's bike with six-packs and head off somewhere, helmets off, to burn rubber. A frequent stop-off for us was Carbeth Inn, a pub nestled between Milngavie and Drymen; then we'd speed off to Drymen, where we knew a great place to go scrambling on one of the guy's bikes, while the rest of us would lay out in the sun, passing the 'dutchie'.

The 'Carbeth' was a serious biker pub with a large gravel area and low wooden benches, surrounded by hairy bikers with their hogs all lined up on display by the road. The A809 is just made perfectly for motorbikes and bikers, with bend after bend of delights.

I remember one Sunday, having possibly imbibed just a tad too much, deciding it would be fun to go scrambling on my GS750. It was not so good a plan, as it turned out.

It became necessary to remove the main stand from the bike, as it scraped on the tarmac on the tighter bends and was a potential hazard. Very bad design for those ignoring speed limits.

Glasgow held a real badass reputation and I feared reaching the end of my year there with a razor slash or two upon my face. The college was on the edge of the Gorbals and this seemed a real risk. In reality, it was a pretty quiet year violence-wise and I only got to witness two fights in those twelve months. Having said that, they weren't exactly 'fisticuffs'. One was a total fall-out in a sub-terranean pub down the Great Western

Road. Tables, bottles, and men were thrown around the bar, and broken bottles seemed to be the weapon of choice that day. Me and some mates ended up bravely facing it out, hiding under the table like a group of ostriches with our heads in the sand, praying nobody would notice us. I actually had an excuse; I was holding a beer mat tightly to some guy's neck, stemming the very steady flow of blood streaming down his back.

The only other skirmish I witnessed was whilst leaving a pub in Milngavie, having left my darling Suzuki GS750 parked at the curb outside the pub, whilst I enjoyed a few 'tinnies' with my then girlfriend. Meanwhile, two gangs of Hells Angels had parked their hogs surrounding mine, and decided to rip each other apart using any type of weapon available at the time. My girlfriend and I casually left the pub having cnjoyed a quiet night out, only to find ourselves in the centre of this testosterone-fuelled carnage, having to negotiate the Angels, all hell-bent on mutual annihilation. How we negotiated our passage, and left untarnished, I fail to understand. More importantly, my GS750 was untouched.

Alas, the year came to an end, and we all had to go back to earning our livings.

Leith

Leith in those days was a fairly picturesque small town on the outskirts of Edinburgh, sat on the south side of the Firth which snakes its way up to Stirling. There were lovely views across the mouth of the river and up towards the Firth of Forth Bridge. I was to venture there a few times later in my career when discharging cargoes at nearby Queensferry. A lovely setting, but not a great 'run ashore' to be honest.

Having carried out a five-day basic fire-fighting course at our first colleges, we now faced the second course, which was held at the Fire Brigade's training school on the edge of Leith. The course in Plymouth had been very instructive, with classroom lectures between refined practical demonstrations and exercises.

We had learned to extinguish fires of various classes of fires, and each was lit in neat overgrown 'barbeques', all in a row. One would be made of cardboard and wood, one of oil etc, and we would take turns using the correct extinguisher on each type of fire. The fires were set out in these 'barbeques' at waist height, in order that we could hold the requisite extinguisher in one hand, whilst not spilling our glass of 'champers' held in the other.

The most gruelling aspect of the course as I recall, was having to 'kit up' with full fire-fighting clothing and breathing apparatus, then run up and down the drying tower trying to breathe normally, and not run out of air to breathe from the cylinder on our backs. I was somewhat fitter in those days; a heart attack would be more of a concern at my ripe old age.

We learnt all about the 'triangle of fire', made up of the three necessary components: fuel, oxygen, and heat. Furthermore, we were trained in which types of extinguishers to use in each scenario: foam, CO2, water etc.

For anyone interested, this is no longer strictly true with the introduction of the family of Halon extinguishing gasses. These gasses are used in low percentages, and once the systems are activated, it is possible to enter the space (for limited periods) and there should be sufficient oxygen to breathe, let alone sustain combustion. Similarly, these gasses do not remove the fuel or heat from the fire. Hmmm . . .

These sneaky buggers extinguish fire without interfering with the fire triangle. They break down the ion exchange which is what the chemistry of fire consists of. Sorry to blow that myth.

It is fair to say that the course in Plymouth had been instructive, but reasonably 'jolly hockey sticks', and civilised.

If the course in Plymouth had been a tad 'Etonian', Leith was 'St Trinian's' on steroids, with a whole Scottish clan of 'Miss Trunchbulls', each being vindictive, enjoying scaring the shit out of us victims. I know, Miss Trunchbull wasn't employed at St Trinian's, but…

No more civilised exercises for us; this was the Real McCoy. Whereas the first course had been about how to fight different classes of fires, this course felt like it had been designed to make us terrified of combustion, and ensure we never were the cause of a fire on a ship; not a bad idea for those of us whose careers were that of tankers.

There were still classroom lectures, but these were interspersed with gruelling exercises, each one designed to fulfil the vindictive wishes of the Firemen involved. I am allowed to say 'Firemen' since there were no women in the Brigade in those days. Sorry, but that was how it was.

Each exercise was done in teams of about six, and involved using fire hoses, which weighed a ton, and were barely flexible when charged. The hoses were extremely difficult to manoeuvre and almost uncontrollable when the nozzle was opened to a jet; the hose taking on a life of its own, like a trapped anaconda.

There was a mock-up ship in the yard consisting of accommodation, engine room, the whole shebang. Fires had been lit by the trainers in various scenarios, and each team would have to manage themselves and organise the fire- fighting. The fires would be enormous and the heat overbearing. We had been taught that if we felt the sweat run up our backs, we were in trouble. Not sure if that is factual, but we were more concerned about not feeling diarrhoea run down our legs.

One memorable scenario was a fire on one side of the mock engine crankcase. We had to enter the engine room from the top level on the other side of the 'ship', clamber down the ladders, cross the grating directly over the fire, get down to deck level, and fight the fire from around the engine. This meant entering the engine room at the highest point, where the air was 'solid heat', carrying the charged hose, then trying to man-handle it down to the bottom plates, without being overcome by it. As we struggled across the open grating above the fire, the trainer would pour some oil from his bucket onto the fire below us. The flames would leap upwards and lick our bodies, toasting our booted feet. If you dallied at this point, you could expect a larger dose of oil poured onto the fire and the resultant fire ball from below. This was beyond an adrenaline rush, and we all lit up fags once the exercise was completed and we'd been allowed back to the outside world. I'm not ashamed to say that I was frightened, and I am certain I wasn't alone in this.

A far scarier exercise was learning not to use water on oil fires. If you've seen the result of pouring water onto a chip pan fire, hold that thought.

We entered a steel room about the size of an average lounge, with a steel bath of oil which was about four metres square. Having donned the full fire-fighting garments (with the exception of breathing apparatus), we each laid down on our right sides, one in front of the other but staggered so that only our faces showed, our bodies covered by the body in front.

The oil bath was lit. There was now a very large bath of oil, about one metre in front of us, alight, and spewing large flames which licked the ceiling some three metres above us. It was rapidly heating up. The trainers used a hose to produce a water-wall, shutting off the one exit from the room, whilst another team lugged in a hose, blasting out a vicious jet of water aimed directly into the oil bath. The resultant explosion of fire sent the angry flames up and across the ceiling, down the back walls, and back across the floor to the oil bath. We had been 'safely secreted' into this last space and so the flames diverted themselves around our prostrate bodies and back to the oil bath. We lay there watching the flames engulfing us for what felt like an eternity, probably just a few seconds.

Not surprisingly we all got minor burns, mostly our unprotected ears. Like most of us trainees on the course, I had grown blisters the full length of my ear lobes, these being very painful, especially once burst and rubbed by my crash helmet. I had come to Leith from my digs in Glasgow on my one form of transport, my beloved Suzuki GS750. I think this was one brief period where I wished I had a car.

I don't recall anyone completing a risk assessment to cover this exercise.

MV Mokran

Having enjoyed a year at the nautical college in Glasgow, we returned to sea to complete our apprenticeships; two four-month trips on ships acting as the junior-most rank of engineer. My first trip was on an Iranian ship, *Mokran* (a twenty-five thousand-ton ex-BP River class product carrier MV *British Neath)*. We tramped around the Gulf loading aviation spirit (for the Iranian air force jet fighters) and diesel (for the Iranian tanks), steaming up the river Khor Mahshahr to Bandar Mahshahr (formally Bandar Khomeini) blacked out, and in convoy.

Maybe the black-out windows and rubberised painted hull should have been a clue. Kharg Island (a frequent port) featuring regularly in the news should have alerted my attention, but no, I was young and invulnerable. One night, radar off, we followed in convoy up the river Khor Mahshahr, into the warzone. This being my third trip, I was well acquainted with general piss-taking. Asleep between watches, the deck apprentice phoned me from the Bridge to wake me up. I naturally was attuned and ready.

"Get out of bed, don't get dressed, get to the starboard side of this ship. We're being attacked by jets!"

"Fuck off," was my considered reply.

A squadron of jets scream overhead. Having quickly realised my error of judgement, I pulled on jeans and ran. What steps would you have taken? Bloody big ones I would suggest.

The money was great. As an apprentice, I was by then on a salary of just over three thousand pounds per annum, but our danger money was sixty-five pounds per day (or part thereof, for a minimum of five days) every time we entered the warzone, and at such little risk for a young guy (it couldn't happen to me, it only happened to others). I recall in a single day entering the warzone twice, which totalled six hundred and fifty pounds! Four months of rocket-dodging was a great way to build up one's bank balance, well-depleted after a year living in Glasgow.

To put this in perspective, I was then on a salary of a little over £3,300 i.e. circa £9 per day pre-tax, and a typical four-bedroom detached house costed around £20,000. I paid-off with just over £5,000 in my bank account, had a great leave, but was £50 overdrawn by the end of the ten-week leave.

Thanks to Maggie Thatcher, sea farers at that time fell into a 'Tax Haven' meant to encourage business gurus into the UK, so our Income Tax was minimal. Being the responsible person that I was, I carefully considered just how big a deposit on a house this would have amounted to when I returned to Blighty. Nah, I bought a modern stereo system, some records, and a fairing for my beloved Suzuki GS750. I decanted the rest at various hostelries around Exeter and its surrounds. Apparently, I had a great time.

The ship was Iranian registered, with a small Revolutionary Guard contingency living on board, so we had to live by Iranian rules: a dry ship, with the risk of being flogged (and I don't mean sold) if found with alcohol.

The Gulf is generally very calm (weather-wise), so we had an aquarium in the officers' bar, which was a very rare thing. One of the fish was some kind of angel fish; angel of death more like. It would kill the other fish from time to time and the Revolutionary Guard were much less than impressed that we all called it Ayatollah.

The *Mokran* had been purchased from BP, and like all BP ships, there was a grille across the front of the bar, that could be dropped and locked at both ends when the bar was closed. The *Mokran* still had this. We discovered that if only one end was locked, it was possible to jemmy the grille and get behind the bar. The ship still carried cans of Export in its stores, so we'd hide a few in the fridge for the watch-keepers to slurp quietly when the Guards weren't in the 'dry' bar. We'd sneak into the bar, wrench open the grille, climb over, close the grille and hide, all with no lights on. Once we were sure we hadn't been 'clocked', we'd open the fridge and climb our way through the beers in the early hours.

This was until I started brewing my own beer from the beer-making kit I had been given; engineer through-and-through. It had to be sifted through one of the officers' wife's tights to rid the fluid of all floaters, and tasted rank, but we'd got one over on the Iranians.

All tankers have a vertical red line painted towards the front of the accommodation and the whole area for'd of this was an intrinsically safe zone. We weren't even allowed to chisel stubborn nuts off of rusty bolts in case of a spark. The Revolutionary Guard had shoulder-launched missile launchers and would fire their missiles at the attacking Iraqi jet fighters from the main deck and monkey island (the raised deck above the Bridge). I wonder if these weapons were intrinsically safe?

Unfortunately, they were poor shots and never bagged a 'kill'. This would have been far more entertaining. No wonder they were called 'Missiles'; 'Hit-iles' would have been a far more positive attitude.

This was my last trip as an apprentice. I was promoted to Junior Engineer part-way through the trip and was now on the princely salary of five thousand pounds per annum. This seemed like a hell of a lot of money and a serious celebration was necessary. I did the honours on my return to Exeter. Actually, I recall doing the honours all that leave.

The Gulf would get incredibly hot. I think it might be one of the world's hottest places. The top plates of the engine room would get to above fifty degrees centigrade at its peak, aerosol cans having to be stored below this limit. The control rooms were air-conditioned but this was for the electronics, not comfort-cooling. I recall cowering under a fresh air vent, the ambient temperature being well over fifty ºC, my boiler suit soaked through with sweat, unable to do anything unless absolutely necessary. Going into the control room would be purgatory, the room being maintained at thirty degrees centigrade and bloody freezing, my soaking boiler suit sticking to me, clammy and like a suit of ice.

The machinery's cooling was provided by sea water via very large circulation pumps and strainers. Watchkeeping was a pain in the ass when the ship hit a patch of jelly fish: the large ship's cooling water pumps taking suction of the slippery buggers. The main cooling system had two sea strainers fitted in parallel with very large 'handi-matic' gate valves to divert the flow through either one at a time. The strainers were pretty much the size of a forty-five-gallon oil drum, with the inch-thick lids being secured by a number of one-inch nuts and bolts. The 'jellies' would get sucked into the strainers and block them within a few minutes. The next hour or two would be spent wrestling off the lids, lifting out the strainers, scraping the rubber beasts off the inside of the large stainless steel basket and into the bilges, chucking the basket back into the housing, quickly bolt up the lid, and vent the unit before changing over strainers; yet again. We'd subsequently go through the process of swinging valve handles, opening and closing valves in a set series, changing over the flow of the sea water, only to start the process all over again.

This work was extremely exhausting and could go on for an hour or more. At the same time, you'd be on your own, having to cope with anything and everything else thrown at you. If you took your eye off the ball doing this, or got caught out by a sudden flock of them, the engine cooling jackets and oil temperature would soar, followed by the auxiliary plant 'dying' and ultimately the alternator giving up the ghost, the lub (lubricating) oil having reached its safe limit. This was frowned upon by the deck officers, who would be woken by the reduced revs of the main engine, and the engineer officers, who would be rudely removed from the bar and have to turn-to and help dig the watchkeeper out of the shit.

This tedium would occasionally be made more interesting when the strainer contained a yellow and brown sea snake, these having one of the deadliest venoms in the world. Wielding a wheel key (an 18" steel bar with a hook, used to move stubborn valve wheels) would be the only solution, trying to kill the sea serpent without being bitten. I'd love to see the risk assessment for this process.

In other parts of the world it would be the same, but a change of strainers possibly taking place only every few weeks, the content being water bottle tops (French ports) and Mersey Trout (Durex).

Off watch, we'd lounge around on canvas hammocks on the top decks, 'bronzying', suspended above the steel decks. God help you if you forgot where you were and stepped bare-footed onto the deck with no flip-flops or towel between you and the unrelenting heat of the super-heated steel plating. It was fun to steel each other's towels and footwear, and see how one would react! We'd fill the pool with sea water and swim around cooling off, with beer swilling around our bellies.

Apprentices

Generally, ships would carry between four and seven engineers on a ship, depending on age/type of ship and its trading pattern. On an older, less automated ship, it would be normal to have a Junior Engineer on watch with a senior watch-keeping engineer. Most ships would have an Electrician on board, although this was not always the case. The Chief Engineer would 'not be allowed' in the engine room under normal circumstances; it being a sign of disrespect if he ventured down below. The occasional visit for a coffee and a fag at 'smoko' was the extent of his being welcomed. Second Engineers would be quite insulted if a Chief entered his domain, the implication being that 2E couldn't cope.

This meant that we had to be a tightly-knit team and in almost every case we were. But it also meant that apprentices had to fit this mould and prove themselves from both an engineering and social prospective. The training was tough, far tougher I believe than ashore.

My interviews for BP comprised of three days in London, with daily trips to 'Big Panic House' in Moor Lane. Around a hundred and twenty of us school lads fighting for a handful of offers for a lifetime's career. The tests and interviews were tough and lengthy, even being interviewed whilst eating a meal to have your table manners checked out. After all, we were going to be officers and there was a formal painting of Queen Liz in the officers' dining saloon.

My father came up to the 'Big Smoke' with me. I'd only been to this city once before on a school trip (to see Chelsea play Manchester United). We stayed at a local Premier Inn and I was extremely grateful to him for his support during those gruelling few days. For all the bad times, he could pull one out the hat when necessary.

Getting back to the apprentices, I guess by today's standards the engineer officers were pack-animals and bullies, but at the time we felt we were simply assisting nature in the selection of the 'fittest'. God, it was fun!

The two-hundred-and-seventy-eight thousand-ton super tankers (VLCCs) were shoved through the oceans at seventeen knots by the high-pressure turbine exhausting into the low-pressure steam turbine; reducing sixty-Bar steam to an almost total vacuum. This meant the production of a lot of steam. In the event of an emergency, two safety valves on the main steam outlet pipe from each boiler would have to be full-bore, i.e. each safety valve was capable of maintaining the working pressure of 'its' boiler with the isolation valve shut and the three pressure-jet burners pumping fuel oil into the furnaces at full power. When these valves lifted, there was a loud explosion followed by a roar only to be likened to standing two inches from a 125-train passing through a station without slowing down. It was a terrifying noise.

Each valve had a jacking lever connected to a long length of steel wire that, via a series of pulleys, were able to be jacked open with a hand-wheel and the safety valve lifted whilst stood some distance away from the source.

If an apprentice didn't meet the grade, i.e. poor engineering aptitude or eating with their mouth open, it was the order of the day to drop a spanner next to the pair of safety valves and get the apprentice to 'go fetch'. As soon as the unsuspecting lad had reached the tool, the valve would be jacked open remotely and the apprentice left to clean up the mess they left behind themselves.

Motor ships didn't have the luxury of such high-pressure steam to taunt wayward trainees, so we'd have to make do with running a steel bar through the sleeves of their boiler suits and hanging them from the crane above the top plates. Being suspended dangling from a hook on the steel ropes, ten feet above the six-foot rockers of a diesel engine, running at 96 rpm, in a swell, with the crane swinging uncontrolled, was a pretty good way to tame the lad.

Like any other industry at the time, we'd take pleasure in sending the naive up into the engine room uptakes (often over fifty degrees centigrade) for a 'long weight' -"Long enough, was it?"- or to get 'steam on the handrails' in colder climes.

High jinks made the watches go more quickly and reduced the periods between being in the bar. You had to be on your toes not to be the brunt of the engineers' humour. If you survived the apprenticeship, you were likely to spend your career working hard but having great fun with like-minded guys, unless you hit upon a patch of steam queens (see SS *British Reliance*).

Sivand

My fourth trip was aboard the Iranian-owned *Sivand*, a two hundred and fifteen thousand-ton crude oil tanker, trading predominantly around Europe. She was manned by a fun and motley crew; a relief, having expected another tub of 'steam queens' after the trip on the *Reliance*. I spent much of the trip on watch with the Third Engineer 'Uncle Albert'.

Uncle Albert was portly, with a ginger beard and bald head, and would deliver all manner of amusing 'salty-seadog' tales throughout 'smoko' during the eight-to-four watches. He really was the character *Only Fools and Horses* had based their Uncle Albert on. We'd secrete bottles of pickled eggs around the engine room, go ashore in France to buy horse steaks. Around the 'witching hour', I'd dutifully take the steaks up to the accommodation and give them a very hot, quick blast under the Breville in the officers' pantry, then dive back to the 'pit' with the steaks.

In the meantime, having dug out a chunk of asbestos from the steam main and stashed a few jacket potatoes in the improvised oven, we'd have baked potatoes with horse steaks, finished off with multiple pickled eggs, washed down with a cup of char. This would be the excitement for the night over, and time to take the log. Fun.

I've always loved playing around in boats: motor, sailing, rowing etc, and thus it was that I was allocated the job of rowing an inflatable boat around the cargo tanks for two weeks. My job was to play boats with two NDT (non-destructive testing) Surveyors, rowing around the periphery of each cargo tank in turn, on sea water ballast, whilst the Surveyors took steel plate thickness readings, trying not to fall into the water. Once we'd completed a lap of the tank, the Mate would pump out the tank by about three feet and off we'd go again. This was insane. Two weeks playing in a blow-up, rowing around a steel box, floating on the oceans, and I was being paid for it!

At some point in the trip we were 'in ballast', at anchor in the Mediterranean. The sun was hot, so what else is one to do? A group of us apprentices and junior-ranking officers donned cut-off shorts and flip-flops, and took turns to jump off the main deck into the sea. In ballast, this was some twenty-metre drop, and with an acceleration of $9.81 m/s^2$, we hit the surface with one hell of a velocity. It was imperative to keep your body vertical with arms firmly by your side and legs together; legs together being very necessary, so not needing to resurface to recover one's testicles.

Once in the water it was necessary to decelerate very rapidly, in order to be able to hold one's breath long enough to return to the surface. This meant opening one's arms and legs a split-second after passing the surface, not a second before (losing said appendages) or a second too late (plunging too deep into the abyss).

Having descended rapidly, there followed a long, long climb back up the pilot's ladder, back onto the main deck. This was a rope ladder which had a nasty habit of twisting; thus, you'd find yourself two-thirds of the way up a wriggling rope ladder, pinned between the ladder and ship's side, many metres above the sea, quite sufficient to burst like a balloon if you fell.

At one stage in the trip we sailed through the Suez Canal from the Mediterranean to the Red Sea. The banks were still strewn with the detritus of war following the Arab-Israeli Suez Crisis back in the Fifties, mangled remnants of tanks and Jeeps etc deposited to rust where they laid; not that rust was a big issue in those parts. These were a poignant reminder of the Gulf War in which many of us had been involved, and all of us highly likely to do so in the future. Manning the ships in the Gulf war zone was purely voluntary only. But it was BP's stance that anyone who refused to take the risk 'could' become unemployable and 'at risk' of redundancy; Hobson's Choice.

The passage was slow and hot. I was on watch part of the way and at leisure the rest. I recall leaning on the deck handrail enjoying the view as we slowly slipped through passage, stood next to me were two wives; the Second Engineer's and the Radio Officer's, when an Egyptian guy sidled up to us making eyes at the women. I bartered and agreed two camels for the Radio Officer's wife; I hadn't realised he was serious, and this took much reverse-engineering to sort out amicably. I'm not sure why I wanted two camels, or what I would feed them on anyway.

Fluorescein

Fluorescein is an organic powder that is orange in colour, dissolvable in water, and shines bright green under UV light. It is used on ships to find leaks in sea water coolers, condensers, and any other equipment which have sea water seals.

We were tied up in Piréas harbour on *Sivand*, suspected a leak in the tubes of the main condenser and needed to prove it either way; and mend the leak if found. Suffice to say that it takes a large volume of steam (hence condensate water) to push three-to-four hundred thousand tons of ship through the oceans at around eighteen knots. This steam, once its power is exhausted, needs to be cooled by sea water until it condenses back to pure water and can be pumped back to the boilers; the process is repeated over and over again for days on end.

Needless to say, these condensers are enormous, with literally thousands of tubes through which the sea water passes, the steam flowing over the tubes and condensing to the bottom for recirculation. Once the ship is up to around twelve knots, a huge scoop drops below the hull and the ship literally scoops the water into the condenser, saving the cost of running the multi-horsepower motors needed at lower speeds. It is possible to walk fully upright down these scoops. Why didn't they do this in *The Poseidon Adventure*?

Some kind gentleman colleague decided it would be funny to fill my boiler suit pockets with Fluorescein at the end of my watch, a manoeuvre I hadn't noticed. The Aegean is a beautiful azure blue colour, so the Port Authorities went apoplectic when the large tide of fluorescent green emerged from the overboard outlet, as I emptied the 'dhobi engine' at the end of its cycle. They piled into the engine room changing room gabling away in Greek at me, presumably asking what the hell I was up to. Looking over the ship's side, I couldn't help but crack up laughing at the ring of bright water under the Mediterranean skies.

    I hasten to reiterate that Fluorescein is organic and does no harm to the environment. No harm was done to our planet in the making of this episode.

Hawsepipes, Fog Horns and Shit Tanks

Health and safety weren't really considered much in those days; one was simply as careful as one could practically be, applying common sense and effecting a repair was imperative.

We were on a fully loaded super tanker (to remain nameless), with the main deck at its nearest to the lapping bow wave, steaming along at a sprightly pace. Deck jobs were sought after (if not dreamt up) in order to maximise time on the main deck 'bronzying' under the sun's burning rays. This particular day it was the ship's Port anchor winch which required our 'TLC' but unfortunately one needed to access the drum from beneath.

In those days I was a physically-fit racing snake and it came to pass that I was deemed the engineer most likely to be able to fit down the hawsepipe, this being the pipe between the for'd deck and the ship's side, where the anchor's shank sits at home when the anchor is raised. There's very little space between the anchor and pipe when the anchor is stowed away at sea, hence drawing straws to 'enjoy this opportunity' wasn't an option.

And so it was I who had to climb down the anchor chain links and into the hawsepipe, until just my head and shoulders poked out beneath the winch drum. It must be remembered that by now, my feet were only a few metres above the ship's bow wave, the bulbous bow scything its way across the Pacific's warm currents. I was under 'pain of death', if I dropped any tools down the pipe: an engineer having to cycle the half-mile round trip to the engine room to collect replacements. The larger threat was losing my footing and slipping down the pipe, getting sucked under the water surface by the ship's movement, spun around, and spewed out by the very large propeller, and becoming shark chum. I don't recall thinking about wearing a harness, or anyone suggesting the idea. Did we carry them?

A ship's fog horn is merely a large kW electric motor with a fan attached, the fan having a volute bell-mouth which is vibrated somewhat loudly by the compressed air when the impellor spins; thus, hundreds of collisions are averted and lives are saved.

On one particular ship, the fog horn motor had given up the ghost and it was my job to get the heavy motor down from the crow's nest, a small platform towards the top of the for'd mast, down onto the main deck awaiting patiently below. Achieving this entailed dismantling the assembly and lowering the fan motor (about the size and weight of a car engine) from the small working platform, towards the top of a ten-fifteen metre steel mast using only a 'sky hook'. We had no cranes or 'chain blocks on steroids' to lower the aforesaid item and we couldn't pop into Handy Hire to grab some protective fencing.

It is noteworthy that the crow's nest is some ten-metre-plus above the inch-thick steel main deck and has two handrails for protection: one at knee height, the other waist height; no kickboards etc, oh no!

I climbed up the vertical ladder, rope around my shoulder; tied one end of the rope to the eyebolt in the motor; removed the holding down bolts; wrapped the rope a couple of times around the handrail; carefully shoved the half-ton assembly off the crow's nest, holding onto the rope for dear life, whilst slowly letting the rope slip through my bare hands, allowing the load to safely descend to the deck below. I'd love to see the

Risk Assessment and Method Statement that justified this operation!

The ship's fog horn was one of the pieces of machinery under a Fourth Engineer's responsibility, certain machinery being different ranks' 'babies': Fourth Engineer = dirty, Third Engineer = dirty/technical, Second Engineer = clean/technical. The Chief Engineer's role was to calculate and hide away his stash of 'spare' lub/fuel oil, rather like the U-boat Captains, never knowing where the next 'Milch-Cow' would pop up. Or they'd nab the bronzy jobs on deck in sunny climes.

But that wasn't the shittiest job I had to do. The sewage treatment systems, or 'shit tanks' (as they were affectionately known then), were of engineering interest and their use was mandatory in law in USA and Japanese waters. The 'shit tanks' were four-stage anaerobic processors, the effluent entering the first stage as raw sewerage, then passing through a course strainer into the second stage holding tank. Here, at the third stage, 'Pac-Man' bugs would chomp away a pump sucking from the bottom of the tank, pumping through an air ejector, and spraying liquid shit back into the top of the system, drawing air with it. The air would enable the 'beasties' to thrive and breed, and ensure all solids are gobbled up 'like a good little boy', carrots 'n all. At the fourth stage the resultant fluid was then ejected (mixed with chlorine) over the side. The discharge was theoretically potable but you'd need cast iron guts to hold this foul drink down.

Despite clear signs in the cabin 'heads', and non-subtle hints in the bar, some wives would persist in flushing their sanitary towels down the toilets. This proved absolutely revolting as we donned a rubberised 'boil-in-the-bag' boiler suit, climbing into the various sections of the tanks to remove them, or unblock the strainers etc.

Whilst working with the Third Engineer carrying out this very task, we'd exhausted every avenue; the only other possibility for the malfunction could be the recirculation pump or the air ejector. We stripped down the pump and behold; there was the offending article, well and truly jammed into the pump suction, preventing the pump impeller from turning.

Now, I'm not the cleverest engineer, but I could see that the Third Engineer's plan to use the compressed air hose was going to end in tears. I couldn't believe my eyes; this was no practical joke; he was genuinely going to use compressed air the unblock the pump. Oh my God, he did! I fell about laughing, in tears, as the towel shot into his face, followed by I know not how many litres of the sea water, shit and piss concoction!!! You couldn't make it up (and I haven't).

Concrete Boxes

Special quick-drying cement was carried on all ships and was a godsend to effecting emergency repairs where finesse would have been futile.

I was sole watchkeeper on the *Sivand* and was on walk-about checking the various parameters around the vast engine room, when I spotted a sheet of sea water spraying from a crack in the three-foot diameter sea water cooling pipe. Being about twenty metres below the surface, the pipe couldn't be isolated other than by stopping the ship for over twenty-four hours with no power, no propulsion, no lighting etc; we had no option but to effect repairs under the best conditions we could make possible.

The immediate problem was to stem the flow, which threatened our buoyancy and stability, not to mention the risk of the leak increasing and flooding the machinery space, or buggering the electrical distribution. I stripped off my boiler suit, hooked my legs around a smaller pipe nearby, laid across the leak with my stomach as a make-do plaster, pulled myself as hard as I could onto the pipe and prayed for deliverance!

I was alone with no prospect of help coming until the change of watch, several hours away.

Eventually I was discovered by the incoming watchkeeper doing his rounds prior to taking over the watch. He called for help and the other engineers rallied around for a splash of the action! They found a large sheet of rubber jointing material and carefully pulled it across the split as I rolled out the way, and then laying back on it as soon as possible. Reams of Tespa Band were then used to clamp the rubber matting to the pipe, more and more bands being applied until the flow was a mere trickle.

Lengths of wood from the Chippy's store were then used to build a make-shift box around the Heath Robinson repair, which was then filled with the 'magic' concrete. Thus the ship continued its life with a concrete box holding the corroded pipe together until presumably the section was replaced at the next drydock.

This repair was not common-place but was not unique. On another ship, possibly *Sivand*(?) we were dropping our pick, when the Mate misjudged our movement. A ship's anchor must be dropped with the ship moving slowly astern, laying out the chain as she goes; it's the weight of the chain that holds a ship in place, not the anchor. The anchor merely holds the chain on the sea bed whilst it is laid out.

The Mate clearly made a faux pas, as the fluke of the anchor penetrated the bow section leaving a rather large hole in the ship's side. Woops!

The space was gas freed, and then we built the appropriate box around the piercing, fitting a make-shift a large (half-metre) washer with a hook through the hull, to hold it in place, then concreted the offending mass; a large concrete zit on the inside of the hull with a hook sticking out of the ship's bow, like an in-growing hair.

There's a certain asymmetry with the Mafia here. We used concrete boxes to prevent sinking and sustain life. A concrete box was a good thing.

Broken Ribs

People often ask me if super tankers roll. Yes, they do, big time! The decks within the accommodation of all ships are built curved across the width of the ship, roughly in line with the ship's movement. Thus as the ship rolls, no point of the corridor rises and falls too much, throwing crew off balance. It was bad enough coping with the roll some days.

The roll of any ship depends on its length versus the frequency and length of the waves. The larger the ship, the slower the roll, but the angle of the roll of large ships can be just as much as smaller ships provided there's a large enough sea. The largest super tankers wouldn't roll too badly in channels or narrow seas where the swell didn't have enough space to grow sufficiently large.

In a large open sea or ocean the swell can grow exponentially, growing huge rollers evenly spaced far apart, and this combination will enable a VLCC to roll every bit as much as a smaller ship. The roll is slow and the ship 'hangs' at the extremity of every roll, lingering, then slowly lumbering into the roll in the opposite direction.

Similarly, ships behave differently length-ways, VLCC's bending about three feet along their length, the bending preventing the ship from breaking its back. I recall such a sight in my early days in a large swell. The top of the forward mast and the top of the two cranes mid-ships would line up exactly when looked at from the top deck cabin windows (Captain on the starboard side, Chief Engineer on the port side generally). On this particular day, the bending of the ship was clearly visible as the tops of the mast and cranes 'chased' each other.

It was in such weather that I once had to make a repair to a pipe above the evaporator, but the only access was by climbing on top of it. An evaporator is a large cylindrical machine about eight-foot in diameter and a similar height above the deck. It operates at low vacuum (hence reduced boiling point); sea water is injected across the heating coils and boiled off, then condensed, thus fresh water is made at the rate of about one tonne per hour.

I was on watch solitarily, working perched on the top of the evaporator, and thought I'd been careful enough not to lose my balance as the ship lazily rolled from one side to the other. I had been lulled into a false sense of security. I fell off the evaporator onto the ship's side. The ribs on my left fell across one of the ship's longitudinal stringers (an I-section girder) and I broke a few ribs as I fell.

We didn't carry doctors and I never knew how many ribs I'd broken; besides, there was nothing that could have been done, even if I had known. So I hobbled around doing my watches for a week or two, digging my fingers into my chest and holding my ribs up tightly to try to make it bearable to carry on working.

All officers had to hold a current three-day First Aid course qualification; the Captain and Chief Steward had to complete a two-week course. The Captain held a large medical book in case of emergencies such as needing to remove appendices or similar, one reading out instructions whilst the other wielded the knife. The Chief Steward was better known for ordering our provisions, selling the beer to the bar, and injecting penicillin into wayward apprentices with needles large enough to administer drugs to horses or rhinoceroses.

For weeks I'd hobble around holding my ribs in an effort to reduce the pain, desperately trying not to cough or laugh. Naturally I was easy prey for my comrades, who found it hilarious to tell me jokes just to see the induced pain. Of course, when the boot is on the other foot …

Steering Ticket

In my spare time I would occasionally venture onto the Bridge and take the helm, whiling away an hour or two steering the ship just for fun. This was often frowned upon by the other engineers, as it meant fraternising with the deck officers; oil and water and all that.

The steering characteristics of different sized ships were entirely different from each other. Whilst the 'small' twenty-five thousand-ton ships would be fairly responsive, the VLCCs were entirely different. A super tanker doesn't respond quickly to its rudder' and it is necessary to be a few steps ahead.

A VLCC needs a couple of miles to achieve a 180° turn, and patience to get it to do so. One can almost turn the rudder 10°-15°, and go off and put the kettle on, and return several minutes later to see the response. It is essential to apply opposite rudder as soon as the ship starts to change course, in order to stop the movement; three hundred thousand tons carries a lot of momentum, and once swinging, needs stopping since its movement doesn't merely peter out.

This way of control is very similar to flying a helicopter but in mega-slow motion. Both require the controls to be moved in one direction, then opposite control applied almost before the initial command has been effective. A helicopter is very similar except that the movements are miniscule, and have much faster response times, and acting in three dimensions!

Having clocked up many previous hours on the helm, I decided to take my 'driving exam'. I got up just after midnight whilst we were negotiating our route through the Greek Islands. I spent a few hours at the wheel, steering the leviathan through the shipping routes and having great fun.

Taking my Steering Ticket was very exciting if not a little nerve racking. I had to steer the ship at manoeuvring speeds up a relatively narrow river (maybe a mile wide?) into mainland Greece. This was bloody hard work which took painstaking concentration, the ship lazily following my commands, then refusing to cancel out that command once heading in the right direction. A veritable game of anticipation.

Having passed my Ticket, I don't think I bothered taking the helm again . . .

Dinghies & Yachts

At some point, I bought a Lark dinghy from an old Sea Cadet friend. A random purchase with no thought as to where I would sail it, with whom, or where it was to be stored. It simply didn't occur to me that my mother wouldn't necessarily want it kept on the drive, with her car stashed behind it in the garage, or on the road.

The Lark was a super-fast dinghy, like shit-off-a-shovel. She lacked trapezes to enable a portly crew to maintain her stability in anything above 'light airs'. She was fun to sail but a handful to those with lesser experience.

Towed behind my 'Guards Red' MGB Roadster, she had great pulling power, or so I thought. In reality, most girls didn't seem very interested in that kind of physical fun at the risk of getting wet, or breaking a finger nail. And so it came to pass, most of my sailing was with my male mates!

Nick and I went to Exmouth one hot sunny day, Lark following MG, looking seriously cool in our shades; hair flowing in the breeze. We were off to Orcombe Point, Exmouth, where we would semi-rendezvous with my mum's youth club group, and sail from there.

Sails up, off we went at break-neck speed, the main sail propelling us off out to sea at a great rate of knots: until we capsized. Unbeknown to me the fibreglass laminations, which made up the hull of the dinghy, had started to come apart through age, and quickly filled with sea water as soon as the boat turned turtle. The carcass lay lower and lower in the light swell, until just the tip of the bows was above water, the white fibreglass giving the appearance of a plastic mini iceberg.

Treading water, holding onto the bow, we looked towards Orcombe Point, which was by now about two miles away, appearing as a thin green line on the horizon. At this point, we both regretted not wearing life jackets. Following a discussion about whether we should abandon the Lark and try to swim ashore or stay with the boat (as my training told me was best), we decided to stay in the water, clinging to the bows, and see what would happen.

After what seemed a lifetime, along came a beautiful old wooden ketch-rigged yacht, some forty-foot long, as I recall. This was the *Fiona K* to our rescue; her owner's friend Pete was out for a potter around the bay. She was normally moored at Starcross, up-river from Exmouth.

I became good friends with our saviour and crewed for him many a time on *Fiona K*, sailing around the South West, sometimes on day trips and sometimes farther afield. I could recount many a tale of our escapades aboard *Fiona K* but there is only room for a few.

The first time I joined her was to sail her from Starcross to St Mawes, near Falmouth in Cornwall, stopping at an overnight anchorage at Cawsand Bay. The tides on the river Exe are extreme, the tidal waters of the wide estuary forced to escape to the sea via a narrow river mouth, resulting in ten knot-plus rip tides, and thus timing for larger boats leaving the Exe is critical.

I duly arrived at Starcross Yacht Club with my 'sailor's suitcase' (typical green canvas with leather corner protectors) for the overnight trip. Pete was apoplectic when he saw my heavy suitcase for an overnight jaunt. What kind of sailor needs this kind of baggage? Once aboard, having heaved on my cargo, he opened the case and a huge grin spread across his face at the sight of so many 'tinnies'. He nearly got saliva on his ears.

We cracked open a few cans and spun sea stories, forgetting we had to meet the high tide to escape the Exe. Having missed that tide, we caught the next one, and the wind took us on our way to Cawsand Bay, where we found a spare mooring, negating the need for anchor watches.

Fiona K was, as I said, a traditional wooden ketch with rusty-red canvas sails, which needed manually hauling up the masts using traditional sisal rope halyards. She looked beautiful carving her way through the choppy sea, black and white hull, red sails, surrounded by white caps dancing on the tops of the waves.

We moored at Cawsand Bay and went straight ashore to The Cawsand, a solitary pub on the beach overlooking Plymouth Sound. From there we could maintain a vigil on *Fiona K*, ensuring she didn't move from her mooring, whilst downing bottle after bottle of Newquay Steam Ale. It was awful, we were locked in, and forced to consume copious amounts of the ale until the not-so early hours of the following day. We eventually staggered back to the tender and rowed back in a wiggly line to our mother-ship, where we crashed into a drunken haze.

I was awoken mid-morning by the noise of other 'yachties' going about their business, so I woke Pete and soaped up, then dived naked into the bay for a natural morning bath - just as the Torpoint Ferry glided past us, the passengers somewhat bemused at the naked bather surrounded by foam, who was clearly equally surprised to see them.

Having not met our timetable at all by this point, we decided it best to go ashore for a quick pint before setting sail for St Mawes after lunch. Lunch became dinner, which became evening, which became lock-in. And so it was, we spent a second night in a drunken state, laid up in Cawsand Bay.

The following day we made a concerted effort to get moving and spent the day ploughing through the seas along the South West Peninsula towards St Mawes. The Cornish coast is beautiful, with cliffs, coves and any number of sea creatures: dolphins, turtles, basking sharks etc.

As we were casually motoring into the anchorage of St Mawes, my then best mate Tim, and our twin girlfriends, were frantically waving at us. We couldn't determine whether they were smiling or grimacing. It was then that I remembered that I'd agreed to meet them here the previous day, and that I'd failed because of our prolonged drinking.

Eos

I drifted apart from Pete over a few years. I was missing the sailing and casually fell into crewing on a racing yacht in the Saltash Wednesday night races. I soon got fed up with the seriousness of it all, discussing a forthcoming race and tactics etc was one thing, but talking about the race all night in the club bar after the race was a stage too far, and I left after a couple of months. To me, sailing yachts meant fun and pubs, not being afraid to move and making the spinnaker collapse in light airs. Personally, if the sails aren't full and the boat not heeled right over, I'd give up, start the engine, and motor off to the pub.

My first foray into the land of yacht ownership was a bit of a disaster. Funded on thin air, I bought a beautiful example of DIY woodwork from the back garden of a budding yachtie from his garden in Cornwall. *Eos* was a twenty-two-foot Bermudan-rigged gorgeous piece of woodwork, but alas not much actual sailing experience had been bestowed on her.

To enable her removal from the back garden in which she had been built, we knocked down the garage. A small crane promptly removed the telephone lines with its gib as it lifted the boat onto the low-loader, the next-door neighbour having his telephone conversation brought to an abrupt end. Off we set to the river Plym to casually lower her into the sea for her Christening. As she was lowered into the briny, the sea water slowly seeped through her hard-chime seams and thus I started the process of pumping her bilges out every time I set foot on her. The mast was too short and too heavy for the small bilge keels, her truncated sail barely moved her in anything less than a Force Four, and above this she became unstable, rolling like a pig in a barrel.

Apart from that, her auxiliary power was provided by a Seagull outboard engine, neatly installed in a lovingly built wooden coffin. There had been no thought put into the design of the engine's aspiration and after a few minutes of running, the exhaust stifled the fresh air (which was recirculated constantly) and the engine would splutter to death.

If the engine cowling was off (most unseamanlike), the engine would continue to produce its God-awful noise and the propeller would continue to froth up the sea in its futile attempt to move the boat in a forward movement. The result of the engine being used beyond half-throttle was the sea surface being frothed into cappuccino.

She lay at her drying-out mooring in Turnchapel, Plymouth. Fully tidal, the choice was to get aboard at either high or low tide. Hobson's Choice. High tide meant stripping down to trunks and paddling out in the muddy waters of the harbour on a Lilo, trying not to splash too much or fall into the freezing, discoloured waters. Low tide meant wading out to the boat in the thick gooey sludge, trying not to step on shit, tar, or syringes, climb aboard, and wait for the 'latte' tide to lift the yacht out of the bonds of the silt, which literally sucked the hull to the planet.

Swans glide over the surface, albeit with legs paddling energetically below. Eos was an ugly duckling. At best, in a Force Four or Five, she would heel over and carve her way at a sprightly two or three knots until the chop would simply overcome the sails, at which point she'd give up any headway and simply allow leeway i.e. slowly drift sideways at the behest of the wind and tide.

Under motor, the propeller would create spume as the cavitation whipped up the surface until the exhaust would overcome the intake, and the engine died an ungainly death.

It was no good, she had to go.

MV British Tenacity

1981-2 saw me cruising around the Far East having an absolute ball; China, Singapore, Australia, New Zealand, Jakarta. Typically, I ended up throwing away many of my belongings when I paid-off in order to cram all the 'gizits' I'd accrued over the trip. I was begging BP not to send me home at the end of my sentence. I was having far too much fun, had spent everything and more. Exeter was never going to replace such hedonism.

Dalian is in the very north of the South China coast in the province of Liaoning, very close to North Korea. It was like stepping out of the Tardis, back in time some hundred years. Old women digging trenches in the streets, open-fronted rabbit hutch living quarters, for all to see your every move in your own home (no printing revolutionary materials at your leisure). Everything was so cheap. I bought a micrometre and Vernier gauge (as one would), and ate like a Lord; king prawns the size of lobsters, and all kinds of delicacies not known to me until then.

A bunch of us bought toy machine guns and it became customary to have wars on board. All ships had a kick-panel in the doors so that you couldn't get trapped in the event of hull distortion or collision, I guess. SAS Commando raids were frequent and it became commonplace to be safely uplifted or taken hostage by a pissed-up group of off-watch officers, who had kicked out the panel in your cabin door and clambered in. Asleep and bleary-eyed, plastic machine gun-toting colleagues would carry out assaults for a laugh. These panels also enabled us to get into others' rooms and deposit live fish into their sea water serviced toilet, which was particularly fun when the colleague's wife was sailing with them.

The handover of watches generally took about forty-five minutes to an hour. The in-coming watchkeeper would inspect the engine room and all other machinery spaces before the handover meeting and accepting the watch. After China, the onus was on the incoming watchkeepers to take over the watch by force. This entailed a full-blown battle with plastic AK47s, chasing around the cavernous machinery space trying to annihilate the duty watch-keepers, who naturally tried to defend the territory. Maybe you had to be there.

One of BP's rules was that the officers' and crews' bars weren't allowed to make a profit. BP had a flat rate for beer across the fleet, and the Chief Steward of the ship would replenish stock at the best opportunity from the 'shit handler' at appropriate ports. The price of the drink was extremely low compared to ashore, and it was difficult to get rid of the profit.

The 'Tenna-City Roadshow' was no different. No, it was the epiphany of ships for booze and parties. The *Tenacity* was built in 1969 and was by now well passed its sell-by-date. She was a work-hard, play-hard ship, with a great ship's company and wives to boot. It was normal to work twelve-hour days just to keep her limping around the Far East, but she was my favourite ship of all. A less tenacious ship I can't imagine, so a bit of a misnomer.

Working on this ship was very physical with little automation, heavy valve swinging, up and down ladders for hours on end in the heat and humidity. But did we rehydrate.

We had to have half-price nights in the bar to try to disperse the inevitable profit we'd accrue, but we'd end up pissed, throwing money across the bar late into the night, unaware that we were refuelling the profits. This would lead to free nights, but the same would happen, the guilt of getting pissed for free just too much.

There were several gay crew members on this ship, two of them cross-dressers. We'd have parties in the officers' bar and invite the crew to join us. Sometimes these two cross-dressers would arrive in all their get-up and one of them was bloody gorgeous. After a skin-full, one had to remember that you would get more than bargained for if tempted. We used to dance with the wives and these two well into the night and early mornings.

Boiler Fire

If you're not an engineering geek, maybe best to jump to the next page!

Like all 'Itty Boats', the control room was at top plates (cylinder heads) level on the port side of the engine room, about midway for'd and aft. Aft of the control room, just back from the workshop door was the boiler. This was a twelve-Bar fire-tube boiler, used to drive the turbine alternator and other steam-driven plant. At sea, the main engine exhaust was sufficient to maintain the main water-tube boiler pressure driving all necessary plant.

Below full revs it was necessary to fire the boiler using a combination of the three Saacke heavy-oil burners. These burners consisted of a fast-spinning cup into which the oil was injected and the result was a burner that had a fantastic turn-down ratio (i.e. the ratio between minimum and maximum possible to burn reliably). Most boiler burners were pressure-jet, and the turn-down was restricted by the minimum pressure required to atomise the fuel in which to support combustion. The downside to low-fire of rotary cup burners was that it was sometimes possible for the oil to track down the cup on the outside and not end up in the combustion chamber.

Fire-tube boilers essentially consist of a water drum connected to a steam drum above by tubes on one side of the furnace, across which flow the combustion gasses from the furnace. The remainder of the furnace walls, floor and roof are made of a membrane wall of tubes connecting the two drums. The water, heated by the flames in the furnace, heats the low-content water in the tubes, which rises by convection into the steam drum, half water and half steam. Surrounding all of this is an insulated casing, and between them the forced-draught fan blows the combustion air, where it is pre-heated by the heat loss from the membrane wall tubes, before entering the furnace, thus saving energy in the process. Over the thirty-odd years the ship had been in service, the Saacke burners had enabled fuel oil to gradually build up between the skins.

It was during a quiet lunchtime at sea, at reduced revs, so that the main engine's exhaust was insufficient to maintain boiler pressure; one burner was on low-fire, topping up the heat input necessary to keep the turbine alternator happy, ergo the pumps running and the lights on.

I was on watch, just finishing a lonely lunch. An alarm sounded on the Decca Isis alarm panel, making me drop my sandwich and dash over to look at the boiler front where the burners were mounted. The entire boiler-front (about the size of a small house) was glowing red hot. Most odd, I'd never seen that before! I dashed back to hit the fire alarm button. I'm quick-thinking that way. Engineers poured down the ladders towards the Control Room, pulling on their boiler suits as they went, bleary eyed from sleep, or sobering up double-quick time. By then I'd dashed back to the boiler front where I was met with a full-blown raging fire, flames licking thirty-forty feet up the boiler casing, igniting all combustible materials within their reach, of which there were plenty.

I was in charge of the watch and my adrenaline was flowing! Immediately the Second Engineer arrived he took charge and being my watch, he and I were the principle fire-fighters, the other engineers in attendance as technical assistants and handing extinguishers etc.

The ship being at 'Fire Stations', the crew were dispatched to do as directed.

It would be easy to jump to the conclusion that the first thing would be to set up fire hoses and blast high-pressure sea water to quench the flames but we were on a self-reliant vessel, far from land. Seawater would destroy the electrical supplies and controls, create free surface effect (anyone with knowledge of the *Herald of Free Enterprise* will understand this), wipe out the lighting and the operation of any electric fire-fighting pumps, leaving the *Tenacity* to waddle around like a barrel with no propulsion or steerage capability. Not an option.

The fire raged over twelve-Bar fuel oil pipes, circulating the life-blood to the burners, heated to over one hundred and twenty degrees centigrade (to prevent it solidifying into Tarmac); should we stop the pumps which could so easily pump the fuel into the flames? Absolutely not. The fuel needed to maintain flow around the system, carrying away the collected heat and dissipate it back to its source via a cracked-open 're-circ' valve. I could ramble on (in my wife's eyes I frequently do) but fire-fighting in a ship's engine room was for me, the epiphany of an engineering puzzle under time and wit pressure, a real test of one's true engineering ability. We didn't feel fear at the time, only pure adrenaline rush, and issue after issue to quickly think through and resolve.

The training course we had undergone at Leith seemed distant, and remote from the reality of fire-fighting on board a ship, particularly in an engine room. Whilst training in Leith, the emphasis had been on the fire and equipment, and had been frightening. The reality was quite different; the emphasis was purely on the engineering aspects, and it was an exhilarating experience.

The ship had slowed down by now in preparation for emergency procedures, a possible 'lifeboat drill'; the ship was a twenty-five thousand-ton product carrier (aviation spirit, petrol, diesel, paraffin etc), and ahead of the engine room was the displacement of an aircraft carrier in liquid explosive. The crew were positioned between the accommodation and down the stairways, feeding myself and the 'Second' the extinguishers with which to fight the fire.

After some four to five hours we'd beaten the fire into submission, but the flames had taken no prisoners and had caused much damage, eating through pretty much all of the power and control cables in their vicinity. The 2E and I were knackered; trust me, that's a long time to work under such pressure. We dived up to the accommodation for a mini-shower as soon as the last flame died, and straight into the bar. The last few hours had caught up with us, and we were both shaking like leaves; too much adrenaline and a spot of fear.

The other engineers and 'Sparky' were left to clear up and re-build the boiler-front sufficiently to get us back underway full-tilt. No peace for the wicked!

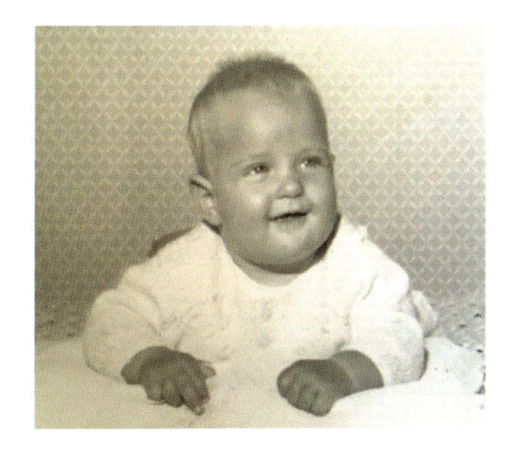

Before my naval inclinations and moving to Canada; and dietary considerations it would seem

"Don't Forget The Honey Mummy"

Gone fishin' in the *Rockies* (1965)

Albert Docks Liverpool 2019

Seeing this building in 2019 was a large inspiration for writing this book; this the building where the *Empress of England* had been berthed in 1964 when we had emigrated

1979 – Engineer Cadet about to join my first ship

Photo session care of one proud mother!

Cato on passage up the Avon to deliver her cargo of Guinness

Captain John Gregory

1869 – 1933

I believe Captain Gregory was the driving influence in my joining the Merchant Navy.

Off to a wedding in fancy dress with friend Tim (Royal Ordinance Corp)

Mombasa and Doris Kamau – I also went on safari whilst in Mombasa

SS British Respect, a 285,000-ton VLCC super-tanker I sailed on twice, and the last ship I sailed on

MV British Dart, the 25,000-ton product carrier I joined to join the Falklands War; but never got there …

My first trip as senior watch-keeper, just out of my apprenticeship. *Sivand*, an Iranian 215,000-ton VLCC

Rotterdam is full of surprises …

But this is a photograph of a calendar.

A rough day at the office!

Disappearing into the depths of the Atlantic – A Perfect Storm

BP Vision

Cool Dude on engine room watch on the BP Vision; by then a Fourth Engineer

Donkey Boiler

I remember my first 'live' encounter with a 'donkey boiler'. These boilers were for starting up the plant from absolute cold, such as coming out of drydock but I'd never seen one in use. I was on watch one morning whilst the Second Engineer and Electrician were trying to get the standby donkey boiler to fire. They struggled time after time to achieve ignition to no avail, eventually giving up and heading back to the accommodation for lunch.

It was time to take the midday log, looking around all machinery, logging temperatures, pressures, levels etc. I was behind two large water storage tanks taking dips when there was an enormous flash of bright white light. I nearly laid an egg.

I ran to the source of light: the top plates. The Electrician was on his knees screaming, his face peeling off in his hands. I was paralysed with fear. I've coped with several emergencies such as car crashes and am fine with blood and guts, but I'm hopeless if I know the victim personally.

I dashed to the phone and got hold of the Chief Steward for medical help, but couldn't speak. I was quite literally paralysed at the mouth. I just didn't know what to say. It was a horrible, horrible experience.

Whilst repeatedly trying to ignite the burner flame, they had been injecting diesel oil into the furnace trying to achieve combustion, but without ignition, the oil had lain in the furnace bottom. During lunch, the fumes had formed an explosive mixture with the air, and when 'Sparky' had tried just one more time; it caused a furnace explosion. He'd been kneeling, looking down the furnace glass (half-inch thick glass held in place with a threaded collar). The explosion blew the glass right off, stripping the collar's threads with it, and the assembly and furnace flames shot into Sparky's face; luckily, he wore glasses or he would have lost his eyes.

Fortunately, we were in port in Swansea and he was rushed off to hospital, never to be seen (or sea?) again.

Lomé

I've been to some amazing places: all over America, Northern Europe, the Mediterranean, Middle East, Far East, Australasia, Africa (N, E, S and W), Milford Haven, Grangemouth, Plymouth, Swansea . . .

Maybe one of the worst places I've been to is Lomé, a grotty dockyard-based city in Togo, West Africa. This was only surpassed by Nouadhibou in Mauritania (this surely is the asshole of our planet?). It's highly likely that Dante passed a colourful two-week holiday there and knocked up his *Inferno* whilst recalling the joys of the Mauritania sphincter. I woke up to the silence of the rumbling diesel, looked out my window to see what delights Nouadhibou held in store, and balked at the dry, dusty, desolate moonscape. It felt like an intergalactic storm had whisked the ship's bulk up to land on the moon and this didn't look like the Sea of Tranquillity. I wouldn't be venturing ashore into this valley of death.

Probably, none of you millions of readers will be from Nouadhibou and I won't have offended. If this book does find its way to WH Smith stores across Mauritania or any other such far-flung shithole, then I'm in profit and who cares!?!

Back in Lomé, the Captain's safety warnings of foreboding death and destruction ashore were passed down the ranks. "Only go ashore if you really feel you need to, and go in groups. Stick to the High Street". How tantalising . . . Myself and a colleague engineer just had to see this for ourselves!

We strolled off into the blistering heat in jeans, t-shirts, shades, you name it. The hot African sun blazed down on us two Whites as we strolled along with dust, rubbish, and foul smells swirling around with every movement. We must have been a rare sight and were stared at by the locals; maybe it was our lily-white complexions, or maybe it was simply *what the hell are those crazy white guys up to?* I would lay odds on the latter.

The 'High Street' felt a bit of a let-down. No pick-pockets, thugs, drug-pushers, nothing. Quite civilised in my experience (then) of Africa. Pah! We'll have a little look down a few alleys for a thrill.

The alleys got narrower, dingier, and far more interesting to us. Eventually we found one sufficiently menacing to tickle our 'adrenaline glands', and sure enough, out popped two knife-wielding guys demanding our money, cameras etc. Two 'Jack Tars' weren't to be put off but we were just young lads; so went to turn tail. Unfortunately, behind us were two guys with sabre-long knives . . . Call us cowards, but we offered them our cameras, watches, shades. But it wasn't enough, they wanted our t-shirts, shoes; now you're kidding, jeans, socks . . .

We were lost, dressed only in 'skiddies', the sun was treacherous, and we had been rumbled. Shame-facedly we had to find our way back to the ship stripped of clothing, chattels and all dignity. The sun was relentless as we slowly cooked under its rays. It was quite difficult to blend in as we shuffled along the roads, white, slowly turning pink, then red, like two crabs in the boiling pan.

Of course, mirth and merriment met our return to the ship, the officers and crew curling up in laughter at our sorry sight (and pain). Sunburn was an easy pill to take; death from a thousand knives having been the alternative.

Jakarta

At some point in a Far East tour (*Tenacity?*) we sailed to Jakarta, a hive of activity on the isle of Java. An amazing run ashore with so much to do and fun to have.

The main roads were about five lanes wide, except there didn't seem to be any lanes or rules; a bit like driving around the Arc De Triomphe, but in a straight line.

It was the monsoon season and, falling out of a club in pitch black, there was a torrential downpour. Having taken it into my head to bum a lift on the back of a moped, slewing across the road and dancing around rickshaws and lorries, I slumped on the back, clenching my bags of dope in either hand, using them to help balance, as you do.

It's possible my mind wasn't thinking straight but I got off the moped at the wrong end of the port, the ship looking very far away and forlorn in the opaque distance. It was then that I spotted the very large pipe running on gallows brackets over the water. I guess the pipe was circa eight-foot diameter, suspended about ten feet above the surface of the water, but it seemed to snake its way around the port towards the ship in the distance. What a great form of transport whereby I could balance my way back to the ship, not getting lost amongst the containers and other paraphernalia. "Do not pass Go. Do not collect £200".

In a fairly laid-back fashion, I staggered my way to the ship (about a mile and a half away), using my two carrier bags as counter-balance weights, balancing precariously along said pipe.

Smoking joints on board needed some engineering expertise; there were two ventilation systems serving the accommodation: one for officers' accommodation and one for the crew. Because the systems both had a recirculation function, it was necessary to share the 'stash' with the crew so that we could smoke in their accommodation, thus not recirculating the herbaceous fumes to the Captain's cabin!

Getting to Jakarta meant navigating the Malacca Straits, then teeming with pirates. These weren't the 'Jolly Roger Ho, Ho, Ho and a bottle of rum' pirates; these were the real McCoy. If in any doubt about how scary these guys were, watch *Captain Phillips* and decide for yourself. Whilst *Captain Phillips* took place off Somalia, be under no illusion that the Malacca Straits were any different in the Eighties.

The order of the day was to complete your watch, then turn-to for four hours, patrolling the main deck with fire axes. The fire axes were pretty good for causing damage and, if you've watched *The Shining,* you'd be lulled into a false sense of security if you thought it would be a good defensive weapon. Unfortunately, the pirates toted AK47s, which top-trumped fire axes somewhat.

We'd walk around the deck with the off-watch deck officer, fire axes bravely slung over our shoulders, eyes peeled towards the horizon (somewhat distant in the dark of night), ready to drop them and run like fuck if a pirate boat appeared. Cricket is a crap game and hitting nine-millimetre ordinance for six is not my cup of tea, no Sir!

Sydney

One can only take so much pleasure, and after some sixteen weeks on *Tenacity*, the time had come for myself and half the ship's company to pay off. We trundled into Sydney Harbour one sunny morning, past the Opera House and on up the river, under the Sydney Harbour Bridge.

The day was warm and sunny, and we were all excited to be at the end of a long trip. We'd spent well over four months navigating the Far East, visiting exotic locations rarely frequented by the BP fleet. The sea and skies were a beautiful blue, we were surrounded by hundreds of yachts with gleaming white sails and powerboats darting around the harbour; the backdrop of the famous Sydney skyline adding to the glory of the day.

Under maritime law, the visiting country's flag and various pennants must be flown from lanyards of the main mast: Bravo (red - I am carrying or discharging a dangerous cargo), Quebec (yellow – my vessel is healthy and I request free practique), the 'Blue Peter' (blue with white square in the centre – ready to sail), Yankee (yellow/red diagonal stripes – I am carrying mails) etc.

Having sailed around the Far East, and many of the ship's company having entertained locals (or vice-versa), we were carrying a large consignment of female underwear, collected from various parts.

I have a terrific photograph of *British Tenacity* passing under the Sydney Harbour Bridge, main mast festooned in knickers and bras, all pennants having been removed. Naturally, half a ship's company paying off at the same time was a rare occasion and very exciting, leading to high jinks!

I recall taking a few bags of russian salad from the officers' pantry and onto the 'paraffin budgie', our plane home. Onboard, the salad was carefully decanted into several of the plane's sick bags, which were then put back into the seat pockets. Once in the air we all took turns to 'throw up' into our sick bags and return the bags to the seat pockets. When the stewardesses came round to prepare for our first meal, we removed our sick bags in unison and promptly ate the 'salad', the more refined passengers around us watching in horror!

The flight was over twenty-four hours including the stop-over in Kuala Lumpar, and I was knackered despite a catching a few *zzzs* on the plane. We also learnt you can get pissed and sober up twice on such a long-haul flight. I arrived back at Exeter St Davids railway station early evening the next day, or was it preceding? My mother was waiting for me in her car, ready to go out for her birthday. I'd paid off and arrived home just in time to take her out for a birthday meal.

Home, unpack, change of clothes, shit, shower and shave, and out for the meal. Slap up steak main course, followed by lovely pudding with custard (or was it ice cream?). Anyway, sleep crept up on me and pounced from behind. I fell asleep face-first in the pudding bowl; not a pretty sight, or cool look.

Christmas Nurses Party

Being away at sea over the 'festive season' could be great fun or extremely lonely and boring. It would be a real lottery, wholly dependent on the state of play at home and the ship's company. Parties on work-hard, play-hard motor ships would usually be wild and raucous, whereas Christmas with some 'steam-queens' on modern super tankers could be painfully polite and drawn out.

We didn't 'do' cards or presents but food and drink were the order of the day, much like any other day but with more of them and not necessarily in that order. I guess it must have been tough for guys with loved ones at home and maybe worse for those with young kids. Self-inflicted.

I don't remember where we were, or what ship I was on at the time, but I do recall being on watch for eight hours during Christmas Day; Billy-No-Mates. We were in port somewhere, probably Melbourne, parties with local nurses were frequent there! The officers had arranged for a group of nurses to participate in yet another party. Its only polite to fraternise with, and entertain, the locals.

The watch went slowly and without event, other than even larger than normal meal portions. Meals were superb in BP Shipping (until the redundancies and outsourcing in the last year), with multiple choices for each course, and we'd often climb through each option in each course, never seeming to devour more calories than we'd burn in the engine room, the work being extremely physical and demanding.

I mooched around the engine room trying to while away the hours, like a caged tiger waiting to be let loose on the punters. Eventually my time was up and I hurriedly 'did the log', a swift handover to the incoming watchkeeper, and up and away to party-time in the bar. I can't imagine having much sympathy to the oncoming watchkeeper, who had had to stay marginally sober before his eight hours.

Before flying out to join the ship, my mother had put a few small Christmas things in my case, and when I got off watch, I dived to my cabin for a shit, shower, and shave, before joining the party. One of the things secreted away in my case was a capsule of fake blood. This presented a major opportunity with the nurses onboard.

Having showered, I staggered up to the bar, 'blood' pouring from my mouth. Within a nano-second I'd got a flock of attentive nurses caring for all my needs (well, nearly all anyway). This was a great entrance and spectacular way of being noticed by our caring visitors.

And a very Merry Christmas to one and all!

Alexandria

As well as two Engineers being on watch, it is maritime law that a ship entering, leaving, or otherwise manoeuvring within port limits, must have a minimum of two generators running in parallel (sharing the load). In the event of one generator 'falling over', the other generator would take up the load, without the ship losing power and floundering.

Not all repairs were of the concrete box type, some being highly refined. We arrived at Alexandria, Egypt, and dropped the pick, waiting for our turn to enter port and discharge our cargo. Whilst sat at anchor, with a poor non-suspecting watchkeeper, one of the small teeth on one a gear within the steam turbine's governor, sheared off, followed by several of its companions in a domino effect. Within split seconds, the lights grew darker and motors slowed down as the stressed-out Engineer tried to get the standby generator started.

'River Boats' carry two standby generators, sat on the bottom plates on the port side of the engine room. These generators were Paxman engines, with a very high power-to-weight ratio when running, but not the most reliable. I'm sure they're great in a 125 or other train engine, but not a great solution for the marine environment. We didn't consider attempting to enter port with just the two Paxman generators and no backup if one or both decided to have an off-day.

The turbine alternator sat there inert, with no means to control its speed and hence maintain the requisite sixty Hertz frequency through the ship's electrical veins. The spare gears had been requisitioned from UK suppliers and were sat in Custom's Bonded

Stores, ready to be released as soon as the ship docked. Catch 22.

Out of desperation, us Engineers stripped down the Woodward governor, removing the offending components. Each watch took turns handing over the batons. We drilled holes where the teeth had stripped off, soldered small steel pegs in their place, and built up the weld to roughly take the place of the missing or damaged teeth. The rough lumps of weld were then very carefully filed down to match the profile of the original teeth, filled again where insufficient weld filled the gaps, and the process repeated over and over until the repairs were difficult to spot by the naked eye.

The repairs to the teeth effected, we rebuilt the governor and gingerly 'ran up' the generator to full speed. Once the turbine had run a few minutes without a hiccup, the generator was paralleled (by hand in those days) and the load slowly transferred from the noisy, unreliable Paxmans, to the sooth-running turbine set.

We got into port okay, and replaced the patched-up parts for the new ones, fresh from the Bond. This was a proud moment for all involved, and maybe one of my peak engineering moments.

A group of us hired a minibus and had a great trip ashore down to Cairo, where we 'did' the Pyramids, Sphinx and even saw King Tut's gear at the Cairo Museum. We decided to race to the top of one of the Pyramids (on hands and knees if the blocks were bigger than they looked from a distance), last one up buying the beers for the night.

The size of the blocks came as a surprise; they reached our shoulders, and the race had floundered before we got going. I guess our Levi clothing wasn't really appropriate for racing in the heat of the day. The camel ride was just as much fun anyway.

We climbed up into chamber of the Great Pyramid at Giza, but I had the weirdest feeling of being 'unwelcome'. Now I'm not of a superstitious or squeamish disposition, and certainly was even less so in those days. I can't explain it, but we definitely weren't supposed to be there, although it was refreshingly cool after the unrelenting Egyptian sun (air-conditioned tombs?).

MV British Dart

I had been touring the Far East on MV *British Tenacity* at the start of the Falklands War. Having heard the BBC World Service shipping forecast a few times- Hebrides, Faroes, Shetlands etc - why would some Argentinian General want to invade a few islands off of the Scottish coast? Maybe just as well I was an engineer, not a navigator.

Most of my school mates had joined the military and several the RN (from my Sea Cadet days). My best mate Dave had joined the RN as a Marine Engineer Artificer and was then on a tour of duty on HMS *Illustrious*, a twenty-two thousand-ton light aircraft carrier. *Illustrious* had been diverted from her usual jollies to head south to do her duty for Queen and Country.

Feeling duty-bound to also do my bit, I phoned BP after about a month of leave, requesting to be allocated a ship which was on charter to supply fuel to the various RN ships and aircraft for the war. I was young, principled, and didn't want to be outdone with war stories of heroism and glory!

I recall telling Mum about my plans over a few real ales at The Devon Yeoman in Exeter. We'd both just completed First Aid training with our respective employers, when some old git keeled over with a stroke or heart attack. We looked at each other and prayed there was a doctor in the house, and Lo!

I was told to join MV *British Dart* at Yonderberry Point, Plymouth, a small oil depot just north of Saltash on the river Tamar. Coincidently, this bay is called Thanckes Lake, (pronounced Tanks). Now this was a godsend. I was living in Exeter, some fifty miles from the ship, and I'd stayed in Plymouth for two years at college. She would be there for about a week having a helicopter pad built onto the stern for RAS operations in the Malvinas. This sounded like a real adventure in the making.

First things first. I got my girlfriend ensconced in my cabin for a few days and had a fantastic time. She literally came on watch a few times. A boiler suit is seriously sexy. I can still see her in the control room across the Decca Isis alarm panel. After a few days it was time for a change, so she went back to Exeter and two of my mates, Manoj and Tim, drove down for a visit. I was enormously proud to be an integral part of the twenty-five thousand-ton product carrier, one hundred and seventy-one metres long and twenty-five metres wide. Beautifully painted in BP's colours: black hull, white accommodation, green grass decks, and Guards Red funnel with large BP insignia.

We went down into the engine room where we poured over the intricacies of the vast array of machinery. Powered by a six-cylinder Burmeister and Wain nine thousand bhp diesel engine, even in port with the main engine shut down, the noise and heat enveloped you as you descended the steps down towards the engine heads. Surrounded by pipes and machines of all types, it was a sight to behold, and I was still only twenty at this time; a marine engineering officer who took full control of all of this, eight hours a day, seven days a week, alone.

We had a boozy knees-up in the officers' bar on the last night. We were to sail around six am to catch the tide in order to navigate Devils Point, a treacherous narrow channel where the wide rivers Tamar, Tavy and Lynher enter Plymouth Sound, generating up to a ten-knot flow. I was on the four to eight watch, so I joined them in the bar straight after I'd showered. They seemed to have melted into the crowd and not too shy judging by the beginnings of slurring.

A great evening was had by all, and I staggered out the bar in the early hours hoping to catch a few Big *ZZZs* before going back on watch.

My alarm went off and I staggered around my cabin trying to get into my clean boiler suit, still worse for wear from our fun a couple of hours earlier. I vaguely remember being slouched in a chair in the control room wolfing down coffee and dragging on fag after fag, trying to sober up and get ready for sailing.

It generally takes about an hour to prepare the machinery from 'cold' to leave port. The main engine jackets are maintained at normal temperature using steam from the auxiliary boiler. This prevents shrinkage of liners and a myriad of leaks from straining seals. The lub oil pumps need starting and full circulation proven; the main engine is turned very slowly by an electric motor with worm drive on the flywheel.

These ships have no clutch or gearbox and if the engine turns, then the propeller turns. This means careful liaison with the deck officer to ensure nothing is trapped and dragged around by the propeller when the engine (and hence the propeller) is turned. Half-inch cocks on each cylinder head allow any liquids (which could settle on the piston crowns) to be squeezed out of each cylinder, thus avoiding 'hydraulic lock' when the engine is turned over 'in anger'. So, the engine needs to be left to turn for a bare minimum of one whole revolution to ensure every piston has been to TDC (top dead centre). This takes five-ten minutes.

Just prior to starting the engine for the first time, the engine is 'kicked on air'. This involves ten-Bar stored compressed air being blasted into each cylinder in sequence, in order to turn the engine over in preparation to start manoeuvring. The deck officer would call down from the Bridge to do this, generally a few minutes before releasing the mooring ropes.

This phone call woke me up, so I guess I must have drifted off, still slumped in the control room chair. It was six am and the ship was about to commence its first manoeuvres in order to hit Devils Point at the highest point of the tide. At this stage in the proceedings, clearly, I'd not even thought about preparing the engine for sea. Our next stop was the Ascension Islands for final preparations for the Falklands War. I was fully awake and functioning within a nano-second. I jumped out the chair and literally ran around, up and down the steel ladders, tweaking, poking, looking, and praying I could pull this off. The main engine having barely done one full revolution on turning gear must surely be OK. I dashed to the Bridge phone and duly announced: "Ready to kick on air". It was at this point I realised the first error of my ways.

Under maritime law, there must be a minimum of two engineer officers in an engine room when a ship is manoeuvring in or out of port. I'd promised to call the Second Engineer an hour before leaving, so that he could shower and dress in an orderly fashion. However, in my drunken state I'd forgotten to wake him. It couldn't get worse, could it?

I rang 2E, who was pissed off at only having a couple of minutes to get up, dressed, and be ready for the fun. I retorted I thought he'd like an extra hour in bed after the late-night bar episode. I'm not convinced he bought this bending of the truth.

2E dragged himself down to the control room still pulling on his boiler suit, while I was juggling the levers to kick the engine over on air. These levers are like smaller versions of the old train signalman's levers for changing the track points: big brass levers with hand levers to engage in the ratchet slots to hold the lever positions. The lever to the left has two positions and selects Ahead or Astern, whilst the right-hand lever has Stop, Interim (to turn the engine using compressed air) and Variable positions to determine the fuel to be injected, hence the power/ship's speed. Feeling reasonably pleased with myself having gone from asleep to kicked on air within ten minutes, I put the kettle on. Over the tannoy came the announcement: "Raise the gangway". It was at this point I felt my knees give way and the world spin off its axis. Second error of my ways.

Unfortunately, what I'd forgotten was that my mates Tim and Manoj, drunk to the full, had collapsed in an empty cabin next to mine. So the ship was ready to commence manoeuvring at any time now, the gangway was being raised, next stop Ascension Islands, and my two mates were 'zonko' in a cabin. I grabbed the phone and gave them a very rude awakening, telling them to get dressed whilst running down the main deck. Do not pass Go. Do not collect £200!

A very lucky break, but in fact no sooner had we cleared Devils Point (by a margin) than we were taken off MOD charter and received orders for Grangemouth, Scotland. I'd given up three months paid leave to fight for Britain, was summarily dismissed and sent on a European tour.

Constanta

I learnt two good lessons in Romania: one, don't get duped with a 'nigger's wad' and two, don't tell someone with a machine gun to 'fuck off'. I'm a quick learner and never repeated either scenario.

Myself and a fellow Junior Engineer (Fifth Engineer in some companies) had a great run ashore in Constanta. It was early-mid 80s and sterling was far stronger than the local dosh, so we decided to exchange our notes on the black market, to achieve a far superior exchange rate than the Captain would dish out.

We were approached by a shady guy and ushered to a back lane where he showed us a whole big wodge of leu, counted them out and swapped them for our sterling. To this day I've no idea how he did it, but when we went to the cashier to pay for our 'gizits', the bundle of leu notes transpired to be one note, with the rest of the roll being blank pieces of paper. A great conjuring trick, but an expensive piece of entertainment for us and a costly lesson.

Mid-80s, Romania was a fairly poor country, a little lawless, and the risk of stowaways high; hence security in the port was quite tight. A jolly Romanian guard, armed with a nasty looking machine gun stood at the bottom of the gangway as myself and another Junior Engineer wandered off the one or two miles through the port towards the gate, Discharge Books (seafarers' passports) in our grubby mitts. I guess the guard was to prevent stowaways but seemed a bit serious.

We showed our Discharge Books to Passport Control, but they wanted to take them for safe keeping. Reluctantly we handed them over and strolled off into Constanta. Having been ripped off (see earlier paragraph), we meandered back to the ship around eleven pm, me being on watch at midnight. The nice guard at the bottom of the gangway seemed quite insistent that we needed to show him our Discharge Books before climbing onto the ship; not as friendly as the previous guy.

Having forgotten to collect our ID on returning to port, we intended to return the following day to collect it. The duty guard was less convinced of the acceptability of this arrangement and pursued the idea that we needed them right then.

Following an exchange of contrasting views, I decided to ignore the guard's demands, suggested he 'fuck off', and commenced mounting the gangway. It was the sound of the machine gun being cocked that made me re-think our position and admit, "You're right, we need our Discharge Books".

This was followed by a harrowing two-mile march back through the now dark port, an enthusiastic machine gun-wielding guard in tow. Not an experience to be repeated and a good lesson learned by all.

MV British Wye

I wasn't ready to go back to sea. My mates had dispersed around the world in various arms of the military, and I was lonely. It had been an okay leave, but nothing remarkable beyond being dumped again.

Having spent the preceding year at Llandaff College of Higher Education, studying to sit the Department of Transport Second Class Certificate (motor ships), I was skint. BP had paid us full salary for six months, and we went off pay for the second six months, but having to pay for digs and all other expenses for the full year. To fail was unthinkable; you'd have to repeat the process without BP paying anything at all towards the course or salary over the year.

Whilst penniless and 'Billy-No-Mates', I didn't appreciate that these issues were merely distractions and that yet again I was sliding into depression. I still don't always recognise when I'm hitting a new spate of depression. Happy-pills offer the only respite. A great black cloud was enveloping me, life seemed without purpose or direction, and once again I felt worthless. What was it all for?

Joining the ship, I bumped into another Junior Engineer also on his way to the *Wye*. He was more junior than myself and had only recently completed his apprenticeship, but certainly was full of confidence and his own worth, in contrast to myself. I didn't hold out much hope of a bosom pal with this guy. To aggravate the situation, I had just successfully achieved my Second Class 'ticket' (Motor); he was unnecessarily green with envy.

Upon joining the *Wye*, he immersed himself headlong up the Chief Engineer's rectum and lodged there for the duration. It was quite impressive to witness just how far one's proboscis can get past another's sphincter.

The trip was pretty much without decent shore leave or respite from the tedium; in fact, I barely remember where we went. I joined in Spain and remember an evening ashore somewhere in Massachusetts; beyond that nothing to tell.

I was on the midnight watch and went ashore with a couple of engineers to 'explore'. We ventured into a local hostelry for a beer and got chatting to a local who worked in the nearby oil-fired power station. A ship and a power station are virtually identical except one has a large propeller on the end of the turbines and one has generators. After one beer we accepted the invite to look over the power station, which was interesting but not exceptional, and got back to the ship a few minutes past midnight. I was late for my watch and the handover from 'Mr Me'. The following morning, the Chief Engineer visited my cabin. 'Mr Me' had reported that I'd been late for my watch, and that I had been to the pub. Of course, I had been to the pub, and had consumed one beer about three hours or more before my watch. The Chief heard none of this, his blue-eyed boy had sowed the seed, and I surely must have staggered into the engine room barely conscious the night before.

The *Wye* had been one of several ships sent down to the Falklands during the 1982 war; they were carrying the fuel for the RN ships and aircraft via RAS (refuelling at sea). An Argentinian bomb had been shoved out the back of an attacking aircraft, but very fortunately had not exploded on impact, but bounced of the main deck splashing into the sea alongside the ship. Upon hitting the water, the bomb exploded and all the electrical breakers were thrown out by the shock waves. The Fourth Engineer had been on board her at the time and his tails of the Falklands were very informative; and scary!

The separator area ('Separator Flat' to us 'Clankies') housed two centrifugal separators: Obi Wan Kenobi-looking machines which separate any water content from the lub oil and fuel oil. The flat had a low deck-head, and this one was filthy, the crew clearly hadn't cleaned it for months, the Second Engineer not noticing or taking them to task on it.

In a dark place, I wrote "Wye Me?" in the grime. The Second Engineer was amused at my sheer brilliance at written composition, clearly not recognising my subconscious cry for help. The 'good old days'.

Piréas

Piréas was a frequented port and I used to love to jump on the train to Athens for a great sight-seeing tour. The Acropolis would look great once it was finished . . . and the mini-skirted army with their 'pom-pommed' shoes were very gay, their 'Marty Feldman' march a sight to behold.

One time we arrived there and got ashore early enough to enjoy a great day's run ashore and visit Athens with its quirky streets and rampant flea market. We straggled back to the launch awaiting us in Piréas, our only means back to the ship. Alas, the weather was bad and the sea rough, far too rough for the launch to get us back safely ensconced on 'mother ship'. What's a guy to do!?!

A group of us went to the nearest night club where the first 'champagne' was free and the sweet painted ladies were very eager for business. I guess the idea was to enjoy the first bottle of bubbly vinegar, buy copious further amounts of extortionately priced liquid and partake of the local hospitality. However, it seemed much more fun to enjoy the first freebie, have a grope, then move on to the next nightclub to repeat.

This was a year or so after the re-gaining of the Malvinas (Falkland Islands), which was still very topical. A beautiful Argentinian goddess approached me and asked me if I'd 'like to fuck' her. Without thinking for a single second I retorted, "You're Argentinian, we already did". Her reaction suggested that maybe I'd found it more amusing than she.

It was possibly in the sixth or seventh club that the local bouncers got together, blocked our exit, and systematically kicked the Ouzo out of us. Not quite the end to the evening we had anticipated.

Dejected and bruised, Dan the Electrician and I staggered around trying to find somewhere to crash, cheaply. We bumbled into a particularly seedy-looking 'hotel' and asked if they could put us up for the night. Now I'm not sure if they'd got the wrong end of the stick, but the first room was decidedly grubby and only had one very worn double bed. "Oh no, I don't think you understand," said we. Eventually we plumped for an even grimmer twin room and locked the doors, paranoid we'd get turned over during the night, the Ouzo now wearing off.

We awoke fairly early in the morning and scraped ourselves back to the launch to see if we could return to the ship. Off we bounced across the maelstrom, up the pilot's ladder, changed into boiler suits, descending into the 'pit' to join the other engineers, now dragging on fags and slurping coffees: 'smoko'. Well, a couple of sips of coffee and the Ouzo kicked back in! We were ejected from the control room and sent back to our cabins like naughty school boys.

Broken Toes

Leisure time seemed to be either action-packed or boring and I became quite good at darts at one point, every ship having a board and 'arrows' in the officers' and crew's bars. My mental arithmetic wasn't great (and still isn't) but if nobody minded me playing with a calculator (to add and subtract, not to throw at the board) all was well.

Some ships would have matches, officers versus crew, or some such championship. One evening we held an officer versus crew match and I was at my peak. I was on the twelve-to-four watch, so had to throw my arrows early in the evening so I could have a few 'sherbets' and sober up for my midnight stint 'down below'. My first dart hit bullseye, my second one did the same. If the third dart had followed suit, it would undoubtedly have been the one and only time I would have achieved it, and I'd have been a hero amongst the officers to boot. Well, the point hit the wire marking the bullseye and bounced off the board. Nil points.

I was gutted and kicked out with my right foot in frustration. Unfortunately, my foot caught the edge of the chair next to the board and I broke two toes! It was excruciatingly painful, and did I holler?

Having hobbled off to bed some while later, I had to pull off the cotton sheets, which were too painful when they touched my foot. I drifted in and out of sleep until my alarm went off and I had to go on watch. My foot had swollen like a balloon and it was necessary to cut the top of my boot into strips to gently slip it over my foot; I couldn't use the laces and had to tie it on with string! In pain, I went down into the engine room like this to do my four-hour watch, knocked up a walking stick, which made me vaguely more mobile, but movement was incredibly painful.

At sea, if you're looking for sympathy, "It can be found in any dictionary between Shit and Syphilis".

As I hobbled around the bottom plates, a posse of drunk engineers would creep down to the engine room, into the control room, set off alarms, then watch, grinning, as I staggered back to the control room to acknowledge the false alarms. "How far would you have got if the alarm hadn't gone off?" One had to play along and laugh, as you knew full well the boot would be on the other foot the next time (metaphorically, hopefully). It still amuses me today, to tell people I broke toes playing darts.

There were many bad accidents I could recount, but in real terms, when you look at the heavy industry we were in, and the timespan over which they happened, I guess our common sense generally prevailed; and not killing albatrosses helped of course (cross fingers).

On all the ships, the external doors on the 'weather deck', and all doors to the engine room spaces, had heavy steel water-tight doors, with a number of 'dogs' around them: the dogs being the lever-type locks to hold the doors tight against high pressures (sinking ship for example). These doors were around 7mm thick solid steel and weighed 'a ton'. In a swell, one had to use the roll of the ship to open and close them; in heavy seas they were difficult to control and close carefully, rather than slam shut.

I recall once, mid-Atlantic in a healthy sea, the Chief Steward fell foul of one of these doors, carefully amputating the fingers on his right hand. At that time every member of the ship's company had to do a two-day First Aid course, (the Captain had to complete a one-week course) for any eventuality, since we didn't carry medical staff.

The best option seemed to be Sellotape. His fingers were duly taped back on, in lieu of the microsurgery facilities that were absent. The tape held well, in that they remained adjacent the stubs, but after a few days they did start turning a strange hue of green and black. They eventually went jet black and rock hard. His party trick became that of putting his hand flat on the bar and banging the beer mugs on his fingers to make an awesome sound and no pain. I heard on the grapevine that he had to have them amputated when he eventually 'paid off' some months later. I wonder what his party trick is now? Not picking his nose anyway.

The Perfect Storm

If you haven't seen the film *The Perfect Storm*, "You don't know coz you weren't there, man".

We were crossing the Atlantic Ocean from the south west coast of the UK towards Boston, Massachusetts in a pretty bad storm and were being thrown around in very heavy seas. Sleeping was difficult and meant spreading out on your mattress Leonardo-style, imitating the Vitruvian Man. Stewards sprayed fresh water on the table cloths and raised the table-edge barriers to catch any plates or cutlery sliding on the whim of the maelstrom outside.

We got wind of two other storms zooming in on us, threatening to engulf us. This can go either way. The storms can either counter each other out and the sea remains relatively calm, or they fight it out and God help anyone in their way. We experienced the latter.

It was winter, minus fifty degrees centigrade with ice and snow building on all surfaces, despite being salt water. The waves, now small mountains, tossed the twenty-five-thousand-ton tanker around like a cork, the propeller popping out of the water periodically. No longer being able to follow our desired course, it was critical that we maintained headway into the waves, keeping the propeller in the water and avoiding the main engine from tripping on overspeed

The weather worsened; the waves grew. The one hundred-and-seventy-one-metre tanker was being thrown around fairground-style; things were starting to look serious. To maintain headway whilst keeping the prop submerged, we needed to reduce the engine to Dead Slow Ahead. It was freezing in the engine room with less heat being given off from the large engine, and ventilation fans delivering sub-zero air to us.

We engine room watch-keepers resorted to wearing layer upon layer of clothing, with duffle coat to boot, sitting on the bottom plates, our backs against the main engine crankcase for some warmth, and where there was less fresh air movement.

One afternoon a few of us went outside onto the starboard Bridge wing to watch the tempestuous sea; it was amazing to see such power in action and we were truly in awe of the might of nature. The ship's bows would dive below the waves for minutes at a time and we almost expected them to come up with a fish, like a hungry seagull hunting. The waves just kept growing; the sea was enveloping all decks other than the Bridge and monkey island. We were taking once-in-a-lifetime photographs of something very few people will ever see or experience.

The Captain was looking worried; when this happens it's reasonable enough to do likewise, and took this as a cue to be 'concerned'.

Gradually but steadily, one wave, growing by the second, hurtled towards the ship. Our eyes bulged at the sight of this green monster, then we ran like hell for the Bridge door. It was comical really, four or five of us squeezing through the doorway, slamming the wooden sliding door shut, then cowering. And then the wave hit us, clearing the Bridge, and went over the monkey island; terrifying.

Without exaggeration, the wave must have easily cleared twenty-five metres, and the ship momentarily juddered to a stop, while it regained its composure and slowly moved forward again.

We eventually made it to Boston under a beautiful, deep blue, cloudless sky; bloody freezing. After our eight-hour watches, we worked a further eight hours on deck wielding fire axes, breaking off the foot-thick ice from the stays of the masts, trying to maintain stability with the growing threat of turning-turtle.

We were carrying petrol and as we discharged our cargo, the ship slowly raised out the water like an elderly arthritic trying to get out of bed. And then the hull, a split in its side, rose out of the water and a metre-long fountain of petrol poured into Boston Harbour; the storm and monstrous waves had split the ship's inch-thick steel skin. We immediately had to back-load the cargo and bring the split below the water level to prevent further leakage.

Having back-filled sufficiently, we turned tail and headed to Gibraltar for repairs. Now to my knowledge, Gibraltar was a port BP didn't generally frequent, so this was an exciting one-off. It was amazing to be tied up alongside at Gib. I'd seen it when passing in or out of the Med, and heard about it many times from my RN mates, but never thought I'd get there. I guess smaller coasters bring the fuel to this part of the world.

After gas-freeing and gas-free certificates had been issued, the dockyard workers were let loose on our empty hull. It transpired that the damage was far worse than we thought. The ship's side was split and she had a one metre slit in her side; two stringers were snapped (one-inch thick longitudinal I-section girders); and a main frame had cracked. The main frame was a real shock; these give maximum torsional strength to the hull and effectively the ship had been breaking up underneath our feet all those miles away. The bow section was completely 'stoved in', so badly that it was concave and looked like a boxer after a bad fight.

Whilst we were alongside, I noticed a Naval Frigate coming in towards the wharf each evening, a small launch going out to meet it; then she would scarper off again across the horizon. After a few days of this behaviour she came alongside the jetty just ahead of us. I couldn't believe it, she was the Frigate HMS *Boxer*, a Type 22 Frigate; my school mate and fellow salty seadog Dave was onboard! I immediately set up a call to him; naturally he panicked since a phone call at sea invariably meant bad news.

"Look behind you! I can see you!" shouts I and a jolly good time was had by all. The *Boxer* had been popping in, and the launch popping out, for these macho sailors to collect their daily mail from home. Bless.

We took turns daily to visit each other's ships and have a good look over their engine rooms and accommodation. The *Boxer's* engine room was very neat and tidy, and crawling with engineers and technicians; like an ant's nest, but very impressive with its two Tyne and two Olympus turbines. She bragged a top speed of thirty knots compared to our nineteen and an acceleration of nought to thirty knots in a couple of minutes, whereas we took an hour or so to get from manoeuvring speed to flat out ninety-six rpm.

Dave was a Petty Officer at that time and I went to view his cabin; it was tiny and had nine berths. The headroom in bed was such that you couldn't raise your legs fully when bending your knees but he didn't have to hot-bunk like they do in submarines. His locker was tiny; where the hell did they put their stuff? In fact, it was more like a locker in a locker, a Russian Matryoshka doll on steroids.

Dave and his mate then came back to my ship for a nosey. We ended up in my cabin for a smoke, the ship then being gas-freed. "How many of you share this room then?"

My cabin was about six metres square with ensuite toilet and shower, obviously no bath. I had a double bed, sideboard, arm chairs etc. We sat there puffing away, chewing the cud with salty stories abound, when there was a knock at my cabin door. It was the Steward come to clean my cabin and make the bed. Dave nearly fell off his chair. This was before I showed him the swimming pool.

Beyond this and the view with the apes from the top of the rock, I remember little of Gib but apparently we had a great time.

SS British Respect

Having fallen in 'lurve', BP kindly issued instructions for my next mission, 'should I accept it': to join the *British Respect* in Antifer, just north of Le Havre, France. I was gutted, head over heels with Anita, and was being dragged away from her for four months; little did I know just how far I was to be dragged from humanity.

Arriving at Antifer after an unusually short journey to join a ship, I dashed for the landline in the pump control room to talk to my beloved. Antifer was totally nondescript, no redeeming features to speak of. Four months felt like forever and I had a deep-rooted feeling in the pit of my stomach; "In soothe I know not why I am so sad".

It could only get worse: orders to slow-steam down to Nigeria to load a new cargo of crude oil at an SPM (single point mooring). This meant a slow controlled 'drift' for two-three weeks down to a large steel buoy, twenty miles off the godforsaken shores of Lagos.

Entering the engine room of a super tanker is like walking into Saint Paul's Cathedral: cavernous. Two boilers sit astride at the aft end of the engine room, each the size of a four-bedroom detached house and more. These boilers operate at sixty-two Bar, the 'wet' steam generated at circa three hundred and twenty-five degrees Centigrade, then super-heated to five hundred and twenty-five degrees centigrade (almost a gas and invisible to the eye), where it is expanded through the turbines. I recall the main steam pipes from the boilers being around eighteen-inch diameter; that's a lot of power, enough to cut a person in half without noticing; a small leak immediately becoming an invisible light-sabre.

The various decks around the edge of the engine room site all of the auxiliary and ancillary plant, and some hundred feet below sit the HP and LP turbines. The HP turbine is about the size of a of Transit van, steam entering at sixty-Bar pressure, expanding through the rows of blades to around three Bar, and develops around two-thirds of the power required to push a quarter-mile long super tanker through the oceans at around eighteen knots. The HP turbine exhaust then enters the LP turbine, and expands from three Bar to almost zero i.e. 0.76 Bar below atmospheric and develops the final third of the propulsion power. This is achieved in a turbine around the size of a two-bedroom house.

Off we set into the abyss, headed for sunny Nigeria. For engineers not on duty, the days were spent carrying out routine maintenance and repairs. This was fine for the first week or two but wore thin on such a well-oiled machine. Fortunately, I then got the chance for some serious arc welding, which I really enjoy.

Following the *Amoco Cadiz* disaster, accentuated by the loss of steerage, BP mandated that raised grating in the steering flat be fitted throughout the entire fleet. The *Amoco Cadiz*, having lost control of her rudder, was unable to be rescued because the leaked hydraulic fluid sloshing around the steerage flat became an ice rink, and the engineers were unable to get near the steering gear to fix it.

The steering flat on the *Respect* was enormous; from memory I would guess it was fifty metres-plus metres wide, reducing to around ten metres at the transom, and possibly thirty to forty metres long; in the centre were the four hydraulic rams pushing on the tiller arms of the metre-diameter rudder post. Enough to keep me occupied.

I was lucky really, I loved arc welding but the result was pigeon shit. I spent two to three weeks welding vertical six-inch brackets to the deck, with horizonal pieces to support the four-foot by two-foot grating pieces which became the new raised walkway to access the steering gear. I remember hours of work, with Phil Collins recanting "Hello, I must be going", imagining doing this welding on Anita's farm. The album still brings back memories of this time.

I met Rob, a Deck Officer Apprentice, on the *Respect* and we became life-long mates, right up until his premature death in 2019. Rob was larger than life, seemed to have an enormous store of general knowledge, and was never far from trouble; great fun to be around! Rob and I courted trouble but we had a ball, or as much of a ball as one could; floating around on a steel boat under the blistering African sun.

In our spare time, we would tombstone off the ventilation casing perched on top of the engine room bulkhead, plummeting twenty feet or so into the five-foot deep swimming pool (much to the Captain's disgust), the secret being, not to break one's legs on the steel pool bottom. Playing darts was another pastime, developing outrageous rules to add spice to the game (but more of that later).

I recall drifting off Africa for months, and us guy's testosterone was somewhat suffering (I think the few women were probably equally as horny). One evening after the beer had been flowing, an engineer apprentice coolly asked the female deck apprentice if she could 'show us her tits'. She calmly lifted her blouse and bra, and revealed everything to all and sundry. She then, equally calmly, placed them carefully from whence they came, and carried on drinking. Nobody raised an eyebrow. It was just a compassionate action by a fellow crew member.

Political correctness hadn't been invented in those days and we made the most of the opportunities this offered us.

Following the trip, I went home for a short spell, then jumped in my MG Roadster, dinghy in tow, and drove off for a week's debauchery at Rob's house in Gillingham. Rob's parents were a lovely couple and made me very welcome; clearly, they didn't know me. I'm not sure which of us was the worst influence on the other, but boy we had fun; sailing in the Medway, Margate fun fair, Med-Sex party (medical Secretaries), and other friends of Rob's. A real motley crew!

UMS

The engine room was so well tuned and reliable, we'd regularly go UMS (unmanned machinery space). This meant the Engineers breaking watch and working day shift nine-to-five. One Engineer would be the watch keeper for the next twenty-four hours, solely responsible for the running of the ship's machinery, whilst the others carried out routine maintenance. This was an incredible responsibility.

As duty watch keeper you would do an early morning thorough walk around the engine room and all machinery spaces to check all was well with the world: no leaks, ominous pressures, weird sounds. Another round would be completed at midday and again between four pm and five pm. You'd then go up top for dinner and a sober evening, ready to do your final walk around at ten pm. After this you were free to spend the evening as you wished (but sober) and get a decent night's sleep, if you were lucky.

In every part of the officers' accommodation were 'Big Brother' boxes with buzzer and lamp. These were a constant reminder that any single alarm would send the duty watch-keeper diving into a boiler suit and down into the pit. It was these 'spies' that kept you on the straight and narrow when it was your duty day, and ensured your vigilance when carrying out your walk arounds.

Once, on the *Respect*, we had a total loss of power including all back-up. I cannot describe just how black, black really can be. To be in a cathedral-sized metal box surrounded by sixty-two-Bar five hundred and twenty-five ^{0}C super-heated steam roaring through the pipes, machinery all running down to a stop, fumbling your way around chequered plate flooring, climbing swaying steel ladders, trying to start machinery, and adjust valves you can't see, is well beyond the realms of exciting.

It took very little to create an alarm situation, and the buzzers made no differentiation between a minor issue such as slightly high salt content from the evaporators, or total loss of electrical power and propulsion.

One very regular interruption to sleep the watchkeeper would get on one particular ship, was at four am sharp; it was like 'Russian Roulette': the gamble of whether you'd sleep through the night or get a rude awakening. This alarm was very punctual, and could lull one into a false sense of security, the risk of this low-level alarm potentially masking a looming disaster recovery situation.

The Galley crew would 'turn-to' at four am, and set about washing down the galley and catering equipment before starting the day's bread-baking. I guess it must have been like the scene in 'The Beach', where the Thai cleaning lady mops down the fly 'zapper' with a wet mop. The resultant alarm would be Low Earth Resistance; the water allowing the flow of current from the distribution system through the equipment, to the hull; earth. There was nothing we could do to persuade the catering staff to be more careful, and we couldn't isolate the alarm in case we masked a more serious situation.

Another random alarm, and one which could strike at any hour of the day or night, was on the *British Respect*, especially when fully loaded (being in ballast gave the watch keeper respite). The two evaporators had a loop on the air ejector outlets such that they were above the waterline when loaded but only just. The result was that occasionally when fully loaded, sea water would carry over and seep back down to the evaporator fresh water outlet and set off a high-salination alarm. Not a big deal to get the machine chucking out pure fresh water after a tweak here and a tweak there, but potentially this could keep repeating, and you could be ascending and descending the engine room ladders; up and down like a 'bride's nighty'.

Tuna

If drifting off Nigeria for weeks on end wasn't enough to test one's endurance, then the worst was to come. We eventually got the nod to head off east to moor onto the SPM (single point mooring). This meant 'flashing up' the plant over a few hours, warming up the steam evacuated pipes and main turbines ready to be able to move the lumbering bulk up the coast.

Finally, with one of the two boilers being sufficient to propel us towards our target at an ungainly five knots, we crawled along under the scorching sun rays until finally 'rendezvousing' with the Nigerian Customs Officials in their launch, ready to plunder our stores before allowing us to moor up to the SPM.

This quite literally entailed these Government employees clambering up our gangplank, armed with machine guns, and demanding possession of our stores. And did they mean business!?! On no, not just a few prime beef steaks; oh no, no, no. They emptied our meat and vegetable freezers, plus all dry stores including all tinned foods etc. Having said this, they very kindly left us with the entire contents of the flour stores.

Having helped themselves to our entire food stock (other than our flour) they proceeded to raid our bars and drink stocks held by the Chief Steward. The bastards took the lot. I'd been hoping they might look a little deeper around the ship to see if we had stashed anything anywhere in an odd crook or cranny.

Not wishing to disappoint, I'd hidden a few bottles of whisky in the back of the main switchboard, right by the busbars. The busbars are made of solid copper horizontal bars to which all the main electrical plant is connected (at 440 volts via switchgear), and I thought I just might get the chance to nudge one or two as they reached to grab the bottles, 440 volts being a little 'livener' for the lucky-dippers. The bottles weren't found. Now this just wasn't playing the game, and to rub salt into our wounds, they proceeded to make us carry their booty from our stores to their awaiting launch! We simply couldn't think of anything we could do to avoid this; they had machine guns and BP didn't care about the losses; provided Customs cleared the ship and we loaded the some two-million-pound cargo, a lot of money in 1983. BP did get it right though, Nigerian Customs sure as hell 'cleared' the ship. Alas my trap was all to no avail and we just had to make do with this as our sole alcohol stash until reaching Europort (Rotterdam) a month later.

And so it came to pass that our pastime of fishing recommenced in somewhat more earnest. Whilst drifting off the African coast, we frequently watched the massive shoals of tuna flashing past the ship, turning the sea into a myriad of colours as the genetically modified mackerel twisted and turned as one body as they sped by.

The huge shoals would move as one and the bright sun would catch the blue, purple, black and silver of their scales as they would roll over in unison, darting hither and thither.

Occasionally a few dolphins would appear, trying to round up the tuna for a feeding orgy. I never could grasp how a six-foot dolphin could catch a four-foot tuna and devour it! Once in a while, one or two sharks would try to join in the fun and bag themselves a tuna or two, but invariably the dolphins would have none of it and frighten off the sharks. A real sight to behold and a privilege to witness nature and the unexpected.

We were somewhat restricted in what bait we could summon up, Customs having limited our options.

Whilst some very ingenious ideas brought what one might think would be tempting to a less intelligent tuna, it was old socks that saved the day.

In the Tropics, the officers obviously wore their tropical uniforms. This consisted of pristine white shirt and shorts, plus long white socks and sandals; we rarely needed to wear our caps, although this would be necessary on the Bridge when a pilot was on board. This get-up was pretty natty and looked seriously good, as the 'scrambled egg' adorned our epaulettes. It was mandatory to wear uniform into the dining saloon for meals, to go onto the Bridge, and a few other times.

Rob was the one to dream up the idea of pieces of white socks to lure the unsuspecting tuna onto his hooks. I have no idea why he would have imagined that a tuna would feel the need to take a bite of his cheesy foot covers, but he hit the nail on the head, and bagged some fifteen to twenty tuna in one day, plus three sharks into the bargain.

Whilst I understand that tuna is quite nice in sensible amounts with a hearty cold salad, we then lived on these tuna and sharks for some four or five weeks until we loaded more stores upon reaching Europort. I can assure you that tuna and shark meat can be bloody boring morning, noon and night for weeks on end, with no accompaniment!

Did I mention just how big tuna are??? Don't be fooled by the size of the cans they are sold in. It would be very awkward carrying tins of tuna the size of human coffins out of Tesco. On average, we were catching five-foot fish, and they are pretty damned heavy to lift onboard.

Tuna are quite literally bloody great mackerel, elongated and more streamlined, but otherwise these are the 'Daddies'. Their colouring is beautiful, almost an exact replica of mackerel. I could possibly write a few lines describing their beauty, but easier if you pop to Tesco's fish counter and think 'Big'.

Killing the caught tuna proved quite a challenge. It was not possible to simply pick them up and whack their head against a solid object; in fact, it was quite difficult to pick them up at all, Sir Isaac's gravity and slippery scales acting against us. We tried all sorts: galley knives, hammers, fists, but mostly to no avail, or too slow a death for the poor fish. Tuna aren't like small fish, and their gazing at you as you pummel them into oblivion is most off-putting. *Inbetweeners* 'gone large' wasn't an option.

Cathodic protection was needed in the cargo tanks when in ballast. This came in the shape of three-foot long inch-and-a-half steel bars with a three or four-inch square coat of zinc encasing them, and a lug at each end to bolt them to the inside of the tanks at intervals. These anodes were incredibly heavy to lift and proved ideal for dropping on the heads of the tuna for a speedy and humane death.

One evening just before dinner, all dressed up in our brilliant-white fancy dress, another tuna fell for Rob's trap, was hauled aboard and an anode duly acquired to dispatch the desperate fish, flapping around not wishing to have been delivered from the drink and plopped onto the ship's deck.

The anode was duly raised, then dropped onto the tuna's head, instantly killing it and simultaneously splattering its brain, blood and guts over our clean tropical uniforms, now a pretty white-with-red-blobs. Time to change. Again.

Boredom was a big issue with only work, drinking, swimming and high jinks to occupy us. Sometimes the high jinks got a little too high. We went through a spate of playing darts for a period. This started off fairly sensibly with the usual Five-O-One game. After a while, this felt a little tame, so we gradually moved the line away from the board, and the distance to throw steadily grew.

As time passed, the rules developed such that the player had to throw the darts the full length of the bar from outside. This pacified us for a day or so but boredom is hard to shake. We developed the rules further to enable the opponent player to have the option of standing by the board to catch the thrower's dart just before it hit the board (or bulkhead). This was a great leveller since it was a good mix of skill and luck: skill to be a good aim from afar, luck to not have the dart caught before scoring triple bullseye. The development of the rules involved regular trips to the Chief Steward for repairs to one's hand.

Eventually boredom grew yet more. The final rules saw the end of the game for us all. As I recall, it was Rob's idea to use fire axes but I could be wrong.

One particularly hot, still day, a small group of us more junior officers took a stroll around the main deck, beers in hand, looking for adventure; anything to give us some form of stimulation. As we were passing one of the deck-mounted cargo valve drives, we saw an extremely large sleeping bat hanging off the handwheel. The bat was so big I thought we'd stumbled across Batman himself taking a well-earned break between saving damsels.

We all rushed towards it in excitement until someone pointed out that it must have flown from Africa and no doubt had rampant rabies; we all retracted posthaste. We'll leave David Attenborough to that shit.

The *Respect* was some fifty-five metres wide and made a great space for recreation. As the days became warmer whilst we glided south down the coast of Africa, we'd play cricket in our spare time, of which we had plenty.

One job for the more junior ranks and the crew was to make the cricket balls: monkey's fists with a large piece of steel at the centre. A monkey's fist is a salty seadog type of round knot; we would have to make a dozen or more throughout the working day, in between our actual work. These had to be regulation cricket ball-sized. It took great patience to make these absolutely round for the perfect bounce.

On Saturdays the engineers would carry out weekly maintenance up to lunchtime, then all hell was let loose in the bar (apart from the poor duty watch-keeper on UMS). Having downed plentiful cans of Export for the afternoon, we'd pour out on deck for games of cricket, usually officers versus crew.

Cricket was a great way to pass time: slow, plenty of time to rest and top up with cold Export and no pointless exercise. The rules were pretty straightforward: a hydraulic cargo valve drive would be the stumps, hitting a ball 'over the wall' was six runs and out. Simples!

Sundays were generally a repeat of Saturday afternoons, except the watch-keepers had changed over at eight am, and it was someone else's turn to get 'gazebo'd'.

Cycling was another fun pastime. We'd race the two bicycles from stem to stern, some half a mile round trip. This sport was cut short when an over-zealous deck apprentice came off on the poop deck, totalling one of the bikes on one of the ship's mooring winches; in retrospect, we should have keel-hauled him.

Blackout

The *Respect* had 1MW steam turbine-driven alternators which were extremely reliable, and a standby 750kW medium-speed diesel generator, to provide the myriad of electric-driven fans, motors and other paraphernalia of plant required to keep us ploughing through the oceans, the ovens to replenish our bellies; and the lights by which to see.

I can't say we really took much notice of these machines beyond run-of-the-mill maintenance; they never demanded our attention like their comrade machines, and it was a case of who shouts the loudest for our attention for much of the time. The turbines continued to scream day and night and never coughed or fluttered, good old reliable capacity to spare. Most machines tended to need 'TLC' to keep them going dependably, whilst others would stop and start in a noisy and theatrical manner.

It came somewhat as a surprise to us when one 'quiet day at the office', the boilers died a death, followed by the main engines slowly grinding to a halt, followed by the turbine alternators. The alternators slowed as the steam pressure dropped and the electric-driven motors died one by one; feed pumps, ventilation fans, you name it. We had a 'brown-out' as the voltage dropped and the lights started to dim; a twilight, sepia effect!

The engine rooms are generally extremely noisy places where ear defenders are essential and conversations generally impossible. My family once visited me whilst alongside in Swansea, and I was able to take them around and show off the engine room: my domain. My mother jumped out of her skin when an air compressor burst into life as she walked past; I could barely contain my laughter. This was everyday life for us engineers, and at that time the engine room was pretty quiet with most machinery shut down.

Slowly the noise reduced as the great monster went into its death throws: the lights dimming, motors cutting out, all steam plant slowing and giving up the ghost.

The *Respect's* engine room was colossal: a beam of about fifty metres, draught of some thirty metres, and full engine room height of some eighty metres, plus ten more up to the top of the flue. Each deck was made of checker plate or open grating, not for the faint-hearted. Long steel ladders connected the decks, and handrails stopped one falling down onto the bottom plates under the roll of the lumbering hull. Each deck was liberally sprayed with all of the auxiliary machinery, with hundreds of valves for the steam, fuel oil, lubricating oil, fresh water, fire main, sea water etc, and which were becoming more difficult to negotiate as the dimness enveloped us.

The urgency to resolve the situation grew proportionally to the dying pressure of the two boilers, and the hue gradually changed from bright, to sepia, to downright dim. I can't recall exactly what had happened (I've slept since then) but I clearly recall the emergency lighting not kicking into life and the frightening feeling as the lights died completely, leaving us in the blackest void I have ever experienced in my life.

If you close your eyes on a dark, starless night you have experienced darkness, not black. The oppressive black of being in a tin box with no opening is absolute, like having a heavy cloak enveloping you. This experience is further intensified when surrounded by the noise of the dying beast: steam being emitted from various exhausts, surrounded by hot pipes, with absolutely no visibility.

Under these conditions we had to find our way around the engine room, find each other, work out what the hell was going on and rectify it, and all whilst the ship lost headway, hence steerage, drifting around the Indian Ocean at the mercy of the great swell. So we staggered around in the pitch black, negotiating the ladders, trying to find each other to discuss what the hell was happening.

I can honestly say this was a scary situation and I wasn't alone in this. Having found the torches we then had to fix the pneumatics system, which was the 'heart of the boilers and main turbine controls', and restart the whole plant from 'dead'. We really could have done with Anneka Rice, since the AA were busy.

Actually, the AA (Alcoholics Anonymous) would have been handy after the bar session that night!

Crude Oil Spray

One Saturday morning we were drifting off the Nigerian coast waiting for the cost of the next cargo to drop sufficiently before loading, the OPEC barrel highly-fluctuating at this time in the mid-eighties.

As I said previously, Saturday routines (when UMS) consisted of the 'non-duty' engineers carrying out the weekly routines throughout the morning, then up to the bar session, followed by cricket matches on deck. I was testing the diesel fire pump for its weekly run using a fire hose, blasting sea water from the fire-main into the Gulf of Guinea, enjoying the salty spray under the blistering African sun.

Meanwhile, the Mate was decanting the sea water ballast (which had settled below the residual crude cargo) using a cargo pump. Now these pumps move thousands of tons of fluid per hour and don't take prisoners. Unfortunately, the Mate was less quick-witted than the running pump, which had now picked up suction on the crude oil floating above the ballast water, having whipped out the sea water seconds earlier.

It's worth mentioning at this juncture, that crude oil is very near the bottom of the fracturing process, only slightly better than heavy fuel oil and roads. Its specific gravity is only slightly less than one. If you picture sea gulls coated in crude oil struggling on a beach, this is a good clue.

The crude oil was now being pumped out of the tanks by the cargo pump and being deposited at great volume under the hull of the ship. Simultaneously, I was operating the fire pump, which also sucks from under the keel, hence the crude oil was then being sucked up by the fire pump and into the fire-main. I was now being sprayed from my fire hose, whilst trying to avoid being splashed with the stinking black crude oil being sprayed around on the sea breeze.

It took hours to rid the fire-main of all traces of the thick, sticky oil. Every hydrant had to be purged of the black treacle; there was not much point spraying this hydrocarbon in the event of a real fire. Eventually we were as sure as we could be that the fire-main was cleared, with only one leg yet to be tested to ensure it was also clean.

I think I mentioned that the accommodation on BP tankers are painted brilliant white and that the *Respect* was in superb aesthetic shape. The final leg to be tested was a ten-inch pipe running at the highest point across the front of the accommodation, with spray nozzles installed under the pipe. These sprays would act as boundary cooling to the accommodation in the event of a fire on the main deck.

And it came to pass, having wasted our free Saturday afternoon on this futile exercise, it was necessary to test this final branch of the fire-main. All was forgiven. To see the whole of the pristine, bright white accommodation sprayed with black crude was priceless; far more entertaining than a few cans of Export and cricket. We had been drifting off Africa for a month and it didn't take too much to entertain us.

MV British Humber

Tedium could be a real issue and sometimes we'd make up the most ridiculous games to while away the hours.

During a particularly bad storm off the north coast of Scotland the engineers made up such a game, that obviously had severe drinking implications. The *Humber* was a 'small' twenty-four thousand-ton product carrier. She was very old, had minimal automation and therefore, because we were sailing around the coast, we'd always have two engineers on watch together: a senior watch-keeping engineer and a Junior Engineer. The Third Engineer and I (on the eight-to-twelve watch) also happened to have an apprentice to torment us.

It was blowing a hooley; the angry waves heaved, tossing the *Humber* around like a cork, the bows and stern regularly heaving out of the grog as the ship pitched, rolled, and yawed; a very unpleasant motion indeed. Imagine living in a bottle floating around in a tumultuous sea.

'Sleeping' entailed laying across the bed spread-eagled, trying not to be flung across the cabin. As the stern was thrust upwards by the maelstrom, the propeller would break free of the water's resistance, spin freely and speed up rapidly. Occasionally, the engine would trip on high revs, the ship slowing down and losing steerageway, the entire contraption tossed around as if a bottle, and the crew chucked around like messages within. The engineer would be in 'deep doodoo' with the entire ship's company when this happened, some being flung from their beds, others spilling their drinks.

The main engine speed was controlled manually from the control room: large brass levers to control starting air, ahead/astern, and engine revs. As the green mountains lifted the hull out of the troughs, and the spasmodic loss of control of engine speed (hence steerage), it was essential for an engineer to sit in front of the levers, manually adjusting the fuel injection; thus trying to maximise the revs to get out the storm as quickly as possible, without allowing the engine to 'overspeed' as the stern lifted too high, or stall when the propeller 'dug in' on the descent.

And thus, the game was born. Each engineer/apprentice would sit at the controls for twenty-minute turns, manually adjusting the controls in time with the ship's movement, increasing fuel as the stern dropped, the prop resistance increased, quickly pulling back as the stern rose, the propeller accelerating as resistance dropped.

The engineer who allowed the engine to trip on overspeed the most times in a twenty-four-hour period would have to buy all the other engineers free drinks – as many drinks as they'd allowed the engine to trip! Simples.

Belfast

Around 1984, our ship got orders for Belfast. I'd not heard of this as a frequented port for BP tankers, and experienced a mix of excitement and dread; this was at the height of 'The Troubles' and we were English.

I guess it would have been around the time my old school mate Tim had graduated with the Royal Ordinance Corps, becoming a bomb disposal 'squaddie'. I know he did a spell in Northern Ireland, remotely detonating car bombs with a mobile robot. Now that's exhilarating!

Belfast is a beautiful city with a gorgeous backdrop of The Divis and surrounding mountains and the people were generally very friendly. The graffiti and fencing around the city were very intimidating and it felt as though danger lurked around every corner. Our English accents were not a benefit to us when talking within hearing distance of 'Fenians'.

We skulked off quietly to a pub in the city centre, mindful of our accents, but all seemed quiet on the western front until the TV in the corner was switched on. The noise of the over-excited football crowd filled the room. The other drinkers all seemed to be transfixed with the match and then we noticed it was Northern Ireland versus England!!! Time to go. "Do not pass Go Do not collect £200".

We skulked out of the hostelry (hostility?) and walked briskly away, not realising we'd stumbled onto the Falls Road. Marvellous. The street sign seemed to taunt us. We felt more conspicuous than nuns in a brothel.

Needless to say, we slunk back to the safety of our ship; the beer was cheaper anyway.

'Vittles'

Like alcohol, food was a very important element at sea and we ate magnificently, until we were all made redundant and the manning agencies took over the staffing of the ships.

We all (particularly the engineers) had very physical jobs and burnt a whole lot of kilo-calories each day. Thus it was our pleasure and duty to devour sufficient 'vittles' to maintain our energy and physiques! Meals for the officers were fairly formal affairs; uniform was mandatory and seating arrangements were pre-ordained by rank: main table for 'four and three-ringers' only. Every officers' dining room had a painting of 'Liz' and we were served by the stewards.

We had a great menu, with a prolific choice of dishes for each course. Most mealtimes the engineers would gorge on a selection of choices from each course, scoffing double that of an average junkie with 'munchies' (allegedly).

I recall one leave, Mum had pushed the boat out and bought us pork chops as a real treat. At the time she was divorced, attending a local Occupational Therapy college, feeding my younger sister, and not 'flush'. Having been used to the usual 'pig-fest' at sea, upon their delivery to the table, I proclaimed, "Wow, that's thick bacon!". We still joke about this misunderstanding today, some 35-plus years later.

I was very lucky compared to many of the guys I sailed with in BP. I had a great selection of different ships and trading routes. Some ships in the fleet tended to continue following the same routes in the same parts of the world but I'd always joined 'tramp ships': no fixed routes or destinations, merely bouncing from one place to another depending on the price of cargoes (which were wildly fluctuating in the Eighties at the behest of OPEC).

Russia, India and South America were countries I never visited, but I consider myself so lucky to have seen so much of the world at this time. Where was my favourite run ashore? I've no idea, they were all so different in so many ways.

Hong Kong in '82 was a great run ashore; only two days there but what a place! Myself and another Junior Engineer went ashore determined to eat as many types of culinary specialities as possible. We ate from street vendors to restaurants. We tried all sorts. I loved the frog's legs until my mother pointed out that the legs are cut off whilst the frog is still alive. We ate all kinds of meats, the most radical of which shall remain secret. I wouldn't like to upset dog owners.

I heard later that a group of the crew found, and ate at, the local Mc Donald's . . .

It was amazing what one would miss whilst away from home; almost like having pregnancy cravings. Milford Haven had minimal pull, unless a trip to Pembroke Castle was on the cards. At one time, I was managing the officers' bar and decided to go ashore to buy some 'vittles'. A fellow Junior Engineer and I went off into the local town to buy boxes of chocolates and crisps, which could be sold at almost any cost in the ship's bar, to support many a half-price or free night's drinking without loss of profit. Newspapers, chocolate, and crisps were priceless treasures.

Having asked for multiple boxes of bags of crisps and boxes of bars of chocolate, I'm sure the dear old lady serving us was convinced she was in the middle of a heist. I guess the corner shops in Milford Haven don't often have bulk-buy customers. This stash would support the bar, and free drinks, for aeons. I wonder if they're still in profit, the ship now having been scrapped and modified by Gillette?

There were pantries in both the officers' and crew's accommodation, where one could brew up or make sandwiches etc if peckish between meals, or trawl when on anti-social watches. The fare was basic: tea, coffee, bread rolls, salad, cheeses, and maybe a few meats, but was very welcome to us off-watch 'Pac-Men'. The engineers in particular could eat and eat like a flock of piranha, desperately trying to replace the quantum of calories burned whilst on watch.

The pantry was also a good go-to place after a session in the bar, when one had 'the munchies'. I recall one such moment, hungry and scrounging food, when I made a large salad roll with plenty of cheese; it looked great. I took a very large mouthful of the roll, and there was the decapitated half a cockroach, its legs scrabbling to reverse from the crevice, and presumably reacquaint itself with its head and shoulders.

The taste was absolutely disgusting: a mixture of radishes and dog shit (allegedly), and was indelibly soaked into the insides of my mouth, and eat or drink as I might, I could not rid myself of the taste of the critter for hours to come. It was foul, picante, and lingering.

Allegedly, cockroaches are one of the few animals which could survive a holocaust; this one couldn't, obviously.

Drinking games were one way of whiling away our leisure hours and of these we had plenty. One of our favourites was to bet on who could drink as many raw eggs as possible, with a couple of shots of gin, without throwing up. It was imperative to drink these concoctions down in one go, and not stop for air, or 'for a rest'. Stopping meant certain vomiting. Six eggs were the generally the maximum one could drink without regurgitation. Now, being married to Frenchwoman, I guess this wasn't so different to eating oysters, which is like downing salty snot.

Another good-fun game was more demanding, often ending in tears (of laughter), and was crazy to attempt on a rolling ship.

Don't try this at home.

A matchbox would be stood on end, placed exactly one forearm's length from the legs of a bar stool. The player would sit on the bar stool and slowly manoeuvre themself onto their stomach, lying face down on the stool. Then began the skilful manipulating of one's torso towards the deck, laying on one's stomach, using outstretched legs behind themselves as a counter-balance weight. Touching the deck was out of the question and immediate disqualification.

Getting to within a few inches of the deck wasn't too difficult, even after a skin-full. But the last few inches always proved extremely difficult to achieve and more often than not would result in road-kill on the bar floor.

It must be borne in mind that all this took place on a moving ship, the deck rolling around at the will of the sea.

I later tried playing this game at our house-warming party, using a standard chair. The balance is all different and doesn't work. I was extremely drunk and didn't think through the mechanics of it. Suffice to say, I ended up falling upside down on my head. Unfortunately, my unsuspecting neck didn't support my body and my face ended up flat against my chest. The next day I was in the Royal Devon and Exeter Hospital. I lived on an airing cupboard shelf for three months and lost my first job, having by then come ashore.

The super tankers often had a cinema and gym etc, all available for our leisure pursuits. Table tennis and snooker were great fun. Snooker, on a moving platform, I shit you not. We used pucks as opposed to balls, obviously.

Table tennis was okay fun, the skill and fun enhanced when the ship was in ballast, and the table at a considerable angle, with the bows being out of the water and the stern well and truly dug in. Playing uphill and downhill added a fun dimension to the game, as did playing in rough seas.

Snooker was played with coloured disks; not stupid these Japanese! (the BP super tankers were almost always Japanese built ships). Again, this was fun, much more fun than in a shoreside establishment, without all the unknowns and unpredictable trajectories experienced on a ship.

Not all ships carried wives, few had female officers in those days (and certainly no female engineers or crew), and parties just weren't the same, unless there were any cross-dressers onboard. One ship carried a blow-up doll; we would dress her, blow her up flaccid so she could sit upright on a bar stool, and squeeze her until her legs shot out in front akimbo; hours of endless fun for the bored.

Sometimes, when asked nicely to do so, she'd dance with us. The Chief Engineer announced in the officers' bar one evening that he had put 'Engineers Blue' in a certain crevice.

Nobody ever admitted to having a blue willy, so this was never proven.

Generally, we were all a pretty hardy breed, and had little time for sympathy or wailing over a broken bone or two. Rats were a real problem and still are, no doubt. Rat-guards were positioned on the ship's mooring ropes when tied up alongside. These are large metal disks that fit snuggly over the ropes part way between the shore and ship, to prevent rats (any rodents) from balancing along the rope and making its new home within our domain. There would be plenty of food for a rat on a ship, with the galley, waste, and all sorts of edibles in the various stores.

A rat was discovered to be in residence in the galley on one particular ship, and it became the engineers' job to deal with the stowaway. We set up a trap with cheese bait and waited for our furry friend to oblige us. Excitedly, one afternoon, the Chef announced to us drinkers in the bar, that Roland had ensconced himself in our trap and would we mind 'dealing with it'?

We dropped our drinks and sped off to the 'killing field', excited and baying for blood. Grabbing the trap, we sprinted to the ship's side, ready to launch the rat and trap into the 'drink', killing the rat for a bit of light entertainment.

Roland was quite cute and at the exact moment the trap was to be launched over the side, we had to decide who would have the privilege. One by one we all declined, none of us wanting to be a rodent murderer. We ended up drawing straws and fortunately mine was not the shortest. Having done the deed, we mooched back to the bar for the 'wake'.

BP Vision

I'd met my first wife-to-be about half way through my four-month leave and although I was in no rush to tie any knots (apart from monkey's fists), I knew this was serious. Deidre (changed name) agreed to wait for me; I explained the usual routine of four months at sea followed by four months leave. Technically, I should have had two-and-a-half months leave, but there were too many Junior Engineers and we were all chasing Fourth Engineer's jobs: dead man's shoes, so our paid leaves were almost always extended. I was sailing with a Second-Class Department of Transport Certificate of Competency (motor ships) by then, and held a Fourth-Class Combined (motor and steam turbine) ticket; a First-Class ticket was only the starting point to be promoted to Fourth Engineer, so my long leaves on full salary were guaranteed.

Before talking about my time on the *Vision,* I must just tell you about her engine. The *Vision's* propulsion was a nine-legged monster diesel, I believe one of the biggest marine diesel engines of its day. This was the only time I sailed with a Sulzer main engine. From memory it was a 9RND90: a nine-cylinder, 90mm bore, Type RND, two-stoke with no exhaust valves (loop scavenged). The curious thing about these engines is that they are Swiss-built. Doesn't it seem a little curious that the largest engines in the world (at that time) were built in Winterthur, in the north of land-locked Switzerland?

The crankshafts, like most marine diesels, were built from individual parts, the colossal webs being heat-shrunk onto the journals. These crankshafts, now solid and some ninety-feet long, were nowhere near any ship building yards; indeed they had to be transported by road through the Alpine passes and tunnels before getting near anything grander than Lake Constance. Only the Swiss could be this eccentric, but such good engineers to pull it off. I can imagine the founder of Sulzer, Salomon Sulzer-Bernet discussing this with his frau: "I'm bored of making dee vatches and need ein challenge in my career. I'm thinking of building unthinkably große diesel engines in the centre of Europe, as far from das sea as possible, mit a few mountains in das way. Seine gute, ja!?!".

I joined the *Vision* in trepidation of four months away from home, but in good spirits overall. The trip went pretty well and life was looking good. On 8th January 1986 I was rudely awaken by the Second Engineer knocking my door down. He barged into the cabin to announce: "You're redundant".

It had been announced on BBC World Service that all BP Shipping sea-faring staff were to be made redundant that day, 8th January, my father's birthday. They had omitted to let us know; it was not long after the 'Britain At Its Best' campaign. A great start to the year.

We were diverted to Venice, another first for a BP tanker to my knowledge. The crew (but not the officers) were marched off the ship, onto a coach, and jetted off back to the UK. An hour later a coach pulled up with a complete Filipino crew. We British officers were very reticent about this; nobody had any experience of Filipino crews, and none of us knew what to expect.

The officers were then interviewed individually by the Bermudan manning agency and offered a job, if you 'volunteered' to stay on board and complete the now extended trip. We could pay off and be flown home with full redundancy pay, or we could sign up with the agency and continue our trip, now extended to six months. The pay was far superior to our current salaries but there was no pay whilst on leave. If we continued to do the same ratio of sea and leave time, the salary would even out. Longer trips or shorter leaves realised a pay rise.

I got on really well with the interviewer and agreed to crew his yacht from the UK to Bermuda on my next leave, the Mate skippering her. I accepted the job on the basis that I had immediate promotion to Fourth Engineer and my offer was accepted. I'd finally earned my first full gold ring

So far, so good. I broke the news to Deidre (my first wife) and understandably this was met with mixed feelings: great to be promoted, but trip extended to six months.

I was very proud to now have reached the dizzy heights of Fourth Engineer and wasted no time in dashing to see the Chief Steward, who would then issue me with my shiny, new, full-ring epaulets and cuff rings. The cuff-rings would have to wait for my equally proud mum to sew them on when I finally paid-off. We were sailing in sunny climes and tropical uniform was the order of the day, so I only needed to wear the epaulets at that time.

Most merchant naval officer gold braid had wavy bands, which is why we were called the 'Wavy Navy'. BP officers on the other hand, wore straight gold bands (as did one other cargo ship company – Elder Dempster?), the same as the Royal Naval officers. This was in recognition of the greater loss of life sustained by these two companies than the Royal Navy during the 2nd World War. Similarly, all Merchant Naval Engineers had a purple band between each gold band; this was in recognition of the bravery of the engineers who sacrificed themselves on the *Titanic*, remaining at their posts, struggling to maintain power for lighting and pumps.

About a month into the final two months of my extended trip I received a letter from Deidre explaining that she had been offered the opportunity to represent England at netball in Hong Kong, but that the tournament coincided exactly with my overdue homecoming. She was in a quandary about what to do. To me this was a no-brainer; we'd only really been 'together' for some two months, the last four-five months of our relationship had been via spasmodic snail-mail, and the odd quick (and expensive) phone call. Who knew what the future held?

It should be pointed out here that in those days, a romantic phone call consisted of the Radio Officer sitting next to you while he battled with his knob, attempting to keep the radio at the right frequency or something. Communication would usually be fragmented at best: the need to press the handset button to talk and released to listen, making things so very natural, and fragmenting the conversation further still when forgetting to press. The voice at the other end sounded like it was the other side of the world (it generally was). And at five pounds per minute, it generally only cost about fifty pounds for a ten-minute struggle to say "Hello, I love you". This was serious change in those days.

Anyway, I was faced with only one option; I 'phoned' Deidre and told her she must go straight to Hong Kong. "Do not pass Go. Do not collect £200". I also sent her the money to buy a new Pentax and lenses, then begged the manning agency to extend my trip a further two months. So now I was faced with an eight-month trip, having joined psyched up for four months and having been made redundant and re-employed.

Scavenge Fire

As I've said, the *Vision* was powered by a monstrous Sulzer engine, a nine-legged two-stroke diesel, the cylinders being 950mm bore and circa 1700mm stroke, three turbo chargers pressurising the scavenge space to over half a Bar, supplying the uniflow fresh air for combustion. The scavenge space was in effect a four-foot diameter steel tube running along the full length of the engine and parallel to the scavenge ports. Each turbo charger was about the size of a Mini.

The *Vision* (as with most BP tankers) had spent the last few years of her life slow-steaming: an early form of ecology (for economy reasons), whereby the ships would run at reduced speeds, meeting less demanding delivery times, at reduced consumption and cost. The impact of this on some engines was not good. The Sulzer engines were uniflow, depending on full scavenge pressures to ensure full combustion of the fuel and the burning off of any residue liner lubricating oil (the oil being injected into the liners as the piston rings passed by on each stroke, thus reducing piston, rings and liner wear). With the *Vision* sailing at reduced loads and speeds over sustained periods, the part-burnt oil would collect in the scavenge space, so you now had a four-foot diameter tube, about fifteen metres long, with the inside coated in half an inch of combustible sludge, all connected to the ports of an internal combustion engine and with around ninety thousand tons of hydro-carbons ahead of this time-bomb.

Feeling very pleased with myself, whilst on watch alone in the early, heady days as Fourth Engineer, with BP *Vision* cruising through the Straits of Gibraltar, an alarm sounded. Holy shit! There was a large scavenge fire and it was my problem!

The only sure way to put out a scavenge fire is to stop the engine, shut the isolation dampers, and starve the fire of oxygen. Not possible whilst navigating the busiest shipping lane in the world.

And thus it was that I had to debate with the Captain, (on the Bridge due to the congested waters) to persuade him of the urgent necessity to stop the engines. Clearly this was not an option, since steerageway was absolutely critical, and I only managed to persuade him to slow down while I applied boundary cooling, praying that the fire didn't spread into the engine room. No pressure then. I was just twenty-four years old at the time and was responsible for the whole situation in the engine room. Pretty daunting.

At some point in the trip we discharged a cargo at Sullom Voe in the Shetland Islands. This was a desolate barren wasteland; the run ashore consisted of the local Village Hall, dosey doe, and Morris dancing. This seemed like real webbed-feet territory.

This run ashore was to bite me in the bum and haunt me for years. Having entered UK waters, my tax-free year wasn't actually tax-free and I was hit with a five-thousand-pound bill from The Inland Revenue (now HMRC), a lot of money in those days.

Singapore Versus Swansea

I went to Singapore a few times but was generally underwhelmed by the Republic of Southeast Asia, finding the neatness, cleanliness and unchanging climate overbearing and oppressive. To 'land-lubbers' it had the exotic call of the East, but in my view it 'could do better; see me'.

After the obligatory sight-seeing and a Singapore Sling at Raffles, there was little else of what one had become used to in this part of the world. The place just had no soul and what little it may have had, has now been squeezed out of it by the 'PC Brigade' and Authorities. I'm not remotely into spitting but even this, and depositing chewing gum on the pavement, was illegal.

Once the tour of Sir Stamford Raffles' statue had been visited, there remained pretty much only the Botanical Gardens to gaze upon. A World Heritage Site, the gardens were beautiful, filled with the most exotic trees, shrubs, flowers and fauna. Jasmine and other flora filled the air with gorgeous scents, giving the eyes a myriad of things to behold.

It was Bugis Street that broke the Singapore mould. In the Eighties, being world-famous for its nightly gathering of transvestites and transsexuals, made it one of Singapore's top tourist destinations during that period. The Kai Tais were Singapore's equivalent to Thai ladyboys and were stunningly beautiful. They'd flock around the Semen ashore, plying us with drinks, looking for a good time. These guys were gorgeous, and it was a good idea not to get 'carried away' when drinking down Bugis Street. The golden rule was 'stick to the ugly ones'; that way you don't end up with meat and two veg, and God-knows-what for extras.

These guys/gals were great fun and we'd roar with laughter through the night with them sat on our knees, telling dirty stories and jokes, the boundaries being understood, and liberties never being taken (from memory). Drinks were cheap and they'd stand their round. I later learnt that the local shopkeepers would line their purses in order to ply us matelots with drinks, so we in turn would spend more in the shops. Who knows? It's all been cleaned up now, the Kai Tais moved on, and Bugis Street is now a respectable suburb. How lovely.

The crocodile farm was the other place of interest to 'Jack Tar' ashore. Crocs, from an egg to over twenty feet, lived here on show to all. These 'dinos' were nuts. Even at four inches long they'd have chunks missing: legs, tails, even parts of their extended mandibles. They were ferocious eaters and would devour anything that came between their jaws, even themselves, if their not-so-flexible bodies allowed. "Look at those snappers".

A croc can jump and thrash its tail to get its dangerous end out of the water to the full height of its length, climbing onto a tree's lowest branches being insufficient to avoid said dinosaur.

They're also fast. I believe a 'salty' can out-run a race horse over the first fifty feet. I'll just take it as read that this is true. Apparently, a racing croc can't turn very easily so if charged, you should stand still, and calmly step aside at the last moment. If you can do this then you have bigger gonads than me.

Now you might think Swansea, of all the world's exotic possibilities, a dull run ashore; you'd be wrong! This was a veritable fun fair and a terrific place for shore leave. Having lined our stomachs around the various local hostelries, we'd always end up at the City Tavern, a night club then-owned by Bonnie Tyler. This place was a blast and made 'easy pickings'. Many a good night a drunken 'matelot' would stagger back to the ship from this joint.

Of course, not everyone could get ashore at night, and so some of the ship's company would have to make do with a sophisticated jaunt along the Mumbles; very pleasant but the City Tavern was far more fun.

Denmark was also an amazing place. The Danes seemed so friendly and a bed for the night pretty easily found. They were great drinking buddies and we had a fantastic run ashore in Copenhagen, Alburgh and Arhus. In many pubs the barman/barmaid would serve you at the table; however, we found it much more sensible to sit on stools at the bar and help ourselves from the taps, while the punters sat at the tables were being served, and the bar was 'UMS'.

The viewpoint of the average Dane then was unlike that in the UK, and I recall Gitte, after a pleasant night in my cabin, telling me all about her boyfriend who also loved motorcycles; okay, that's weird (or is it?). I thought the Danes were Great!

SS British Respect

The *Respect* was a 'beautiful' ship, well-maintained, and a joy to be part of. She was built by Mitsubishi Heavy Industries, every nut and bolt. The builders had put a lot of thought into her construction: easy access to all plant, commonality of parts. Even the fridge and kettle in the pantries were built by MHI.

Whilst my main qualification was in motor ships (large diesel engines or 'Stone Crushers'), I also sailed on steam turbine-powered ships and I had a real affection for *British Respect*.

It was with great excitement that in '86, at the end of my leave, I received the phone call from BP Shipping informing me I was to join her out in Nagoya, Japan. My instructions were to fly to Osaka, sleep overnight at a hotel, catch a Bullet Train the following day to Nagoya train station, and be escorted to the join ship. Wow! Incredible, after nearly ten years with BP I'd finally got a trip to Japan. I was revved up and ready to go. I had the presence of mind to ask BP to send me out to Osaka a few days early, and I would stump up the hotel and food expenses.

Thus, I flew out one sunny day to Japan, flying high above Alaska without a cloud in the sky. This was probably the most beautiful sight I'd seen from the air: tall white jagged mountains, the whole vista covered in icing sugar. Crossing the Dateline, this was the most exhausting and disarranging flights I'd ever taken.

Early evening I duly arrived at the terribly nice hotel as planned, so I figured a quick beer, dinner, and early night were in store, and a hard day's sight-seeing to follow. All terribly well thought out.

A quick shower and change of clothes, totally confused as to what day it was, I ventured to the bar and tucked into a well-deserved pint, followed by a few more. I got chatting to a local young lady, who decided I needed her as a guide; she seemed to think I needed to visit Nagasaki with her and to see the shadows of the fried locals from 1945, and she said she'd pick me up from my hotel room at nine am the following day; so far so good!

At some point she left to get her beauty sleep ready for the next day, and a few pints later I got chatting to a local guy, who wanted to show me the sights at a few local pubs. Not being one to be impolite, I naturally went off with him, barely understanding half of what he said. It proved a good move as he owned several pubs in the city and we spent the night pub crawling, literally crawling.

Karaoke hadn't reached the UK at this time, so I really hadn't been prepared for the night to come. Now I'm a really poor singer at the best of times; in fact, my primary school music teacher, Mr Middleton, asked me not to join the school choir (I was devastated and psychologically damaged for life). Nevertheless, the Japanese hadn't progressed from the Beatles and I literally sang for my supper, staggering back to my hotel room around seven am, absolutely 'gazeboed'. It had been a hard day's night.

At what was (probably) precisely nine am the young Japanese lady arrived at the desk of the hotel concierge, who then tried to call me, but I wasn't conscious. Sometime later I was awakened by someone banging on my door, and I just about managed to grope my way to open it. It was my drinking buddy; his bars were awaiting another onslaught, so after a quick shower, shit, and shave, I followed on to recommence my solo career impersonating the 'famous quartet', badly.

I've no idea how I managed it, but I carried on until the not-so-early hours the following morning. What seemed like minutes later, my door was knocked on again. It was the Concierge come to explain to me about Japanese customs and integrity, and that I'd truly insulted a young Japanese lady by standing her up; just as well she didn't live in the UK. Furthermore, my taxi for the train station was outside waiting for me.

A second frantic shower, shit, and shave, then I ran down to the street below to embark on my journey to Nagoya.

The train was 'tidy' (for my Welsh mates), with waiters and waitresses regularly coming around with steaming hot towels to wipe away the sticky sweat haemorrhaging from our pores. The journey was entrancing with miles of multi-tiered paddy fields, luscious green mountains and generally picture-book scenery.

And then I arrived at Nagoya to be met by a ship's agent and whisked off to join the two-hundred and seventy-eight-thousand-ton VLCC. I was on watch pretty much as soon as I arrived; grab a boiler suit and down the pit!

Having sailed on her previously, I felt I knew her backwards and loved watch-keeping, being in sole charge of the finely-tuned machinery. I even recognised certain signature noises such as the low scream of the turbine cross-over valve letting by. I instinctively knew whether to tweak the valve open or closed by the sound (understanding by the noise which way the steam was moving). The steam pressure between the HP and LP turbines was at three Bar, and below certain power we would feed live steam into the cross-over pipe to just boost the LP turbine power output. Above this level we'd bleed the three-Bar steam and use it to produce fresh water: boiled sea water at low pressure, heated to boil off and condense, to make boiler make-up feed or potable water.

The noise is incredible, with machines pumping high pressure water and fuel, steam turbine pumps, generators, and any number of other plant. It can be quite intimidating to behold, and even more intimidating to be in sole charge of it all at my then ripe age.

Having been onboard less than an hour, I descended the ladders into the bowels of the ship to take charge of the watch. Cargo was soon to be pumped out ashore via the steam turbine-driven cargo pumps and out through the three-foot diameter cargo pipes, all five of them. Before this could commence, the Mate on deck watch had to decant out the few inches of sea water from under the cargo. In fact, the term decanting is misleading; it is in fact pumped out.

I received the phone call from the Mate requesting one of the cargo pumps be run up to speed (started). This entailed descending the ladders to the bottom plates at the for'd end of the engine room where the five turbines resided, the pumps being in an adjacent machinery space driven by the turbines through a gas-tight shaft seal.

Starting the pumps is a potentially dangerous procedure whereby sixty-two Bar super-heated steam is used to drive these turbines. Great care must be taken to start the pumps slowly to ensure no slugs of condensate shoot down the pipes and strip the blades in an explosion. There was a ship in the fleet with turbine blades still embedded in the deckhead where such care had not been taken.

I got down to the pump turbine and saw that it was turning slowly in the wrong direction. I'd never seen this before, the pump always being stationary until started. It was only because of previous experience and intuition that I realised the pump was turning backwards: clockwise, not anti-clockwise, as was the norm. Slightly bemused, I opened the steam valve carefully, bringing the pump to a standstill, then rotating it slowly anti-clockwise.

Leaving the pump ticking over slowly, I phoned the Mate to find out what was going on. He was apoplectic, screaming obscenities at me and generally out of control. Within a few minutes there was a bunch of Japanese guys coming for me. I was arrested by the Port Authorities, and the ship impounded.

Apparently whilst decanting, we had inadvertently pumped about two hundred tons of crude oil into Nagoya harbour. Allegedly it was my doing, having supposedly 'started the steam turbine in the wrong direction'.

After several days of interrogation by the Japanese Authorities with an interpreter to assist me, I'd raised enough doubt to have the ship fully impounded and a formal court case instigated. I was under house-arrest, confined to the ship, with the possibility of a stiff sentence in a Japanese prison looming over me. I was terrified and had visions of *Tenko*: being tortured, with bamboo shoots being grown through my torso.

As the case progressed, more and more professional witnesses were called. The Chief Marine Superintendent from BP was flown out from the UK, engineer witnesses from the turbine and pump manufacturers were flown in from wherever, culminating in a court case in Nagoya, with the Mate and myself at the heart of it.

The Mate in his mid-fifties and I was twenty-four; obviously it was my mistake and I was at fault. A charge of gross misconduct and a prison sentence hung over me. My translator did the best he could and I was duly instructed to sign my witness statement, written in Japanese hieroglyphics. Was this a stitch-up? I explained as best as I could that it was impossible to start a turbine in the wrong direction, unless you had the suck of a Dyson.

The various professional witnesses agreed with my explanations; I was exonerated and was cordially thanked by the Judge for reacting the way I did, thereby preventing a larger scale catastrophe for Japan. It transpired that a non-return valve was partly to blame but the Mate hadn't reacted correctly and was given a twenty-thousand-pound fine, a lot of money in the early Eighties.

This whole debacle lasted an entire week and was probably one of the longest weeks of my memory i.e. the last two days.

Having discharged our cargo the following week, we set sail. Now, a tanker has bilge keels: small 'fins' that run along the curve of the hull, and a great deal of crude oil had sat festering there since our faux pas. As the ship slipped out of port across the horizon, so crude oil drifted out from its resting place and popped up to the surface. A helicopter followed us for two days watching for further contamination of Japanese waters, at what cost!?!

The engine room pipes had grown strategically place 'daisy's' since my last trip on her. I now realise these were standard thermocouples and transducers with which to read temperatures and pressures. Instead of carrying a notepad and pen to collect the information for the end-of-watch log, we would carry a 'box' with a digital read-out screen around our necks with which to take the readings. This was really strange and new to us, and made it slightly longer to do the rounds. However, the Chief Engineer could feed the information to a new, bigger box, which had a screen, keyboard and mouse; I'd never heard of, let alone seen a personal computer before. This 'box' would spit out the thermal efficiency of the entire steam plant within a few minutes; a job which would have taken an hour or so previously, being done by calculation by the Chief (and open to human error).

There was another of these 'wonder boxes' in the ship's officer's common office for all officers to use at leisure in their spare time. It was limited to a few very basic games such as Connect Four; youngers will need to Google this! I used it once with Taff, then lost interest; it would never catch on. Personal computers and the internet exploded into our lives a decade later.

The radar on the bridge was 'space age' also. The ship's course would follow any china graph pencil line drawn on the screen, and an alarm sound if the ship went of course and crossed outer lines on the radar screen (also drawn by china graph pencil). This was surely magical.

Such technology was incredible to us then, and it felt as though we were manning the *USS Enterprise* rather than a 'modern' super tanker.

Respect was my last trip on a BP tanker. She was on charter to the Iranians, on Lightening duties. This was a spectacularly dangerous occupation, generally consisting of loading our cargo in war-torn ports such as Kharg Island, steaming to the mouth of the Gulf (Straits of Hormuz) and discharging the cargo onto a ship tied up alongside, the recipient vessel not being insured to go into the war zone.

I had joined her for a seven-month trip.

We'd frequented all the usual beauty spots: Hormuz, Siri Island, Bandar Mahshahr, Bandar Abbas, Bahrain, Kuwait, Abu Dhabi, Kharg Island . . .

The ship's hull was painted in thick, rubberised paint which absorbed radar, and there was a frame welded to the hull around the engine room, from which hung a steel mesh net. Supposedly, the net was to get the heat-seeking Exocet missiles to explode just before they entered the engine room, killing everyone in there. The Exocets make a very large bang but it's the fuel they carry that does the real damage. I guess there was a clue as to the dangers, from just looking at the ship.

The bulk of the trip held just the usual risks: being randomly attacked by Iranian missiles, fired from miles away, with no real idea of their target and minimal chance of a hit. Iraqi bombardment was also regularly on the menu. The Iraqis were the much higher risk but their border was sufficiently far away that they could barely reach us; but they could at a stretch.

We then found out that the Iraqis had bought a 'flock' of Mirage jets and were now using laser-guided bombs. This changed everything for us, the odds against us having multiplied at a stroke. Mirage jets can be refuelled in the air and we were no longer outside of their range. The use of laser-guided bombs at short range meant almost certain hits and no longer being able to hope the missile's fuel would be low. This simply wasn't playing the game and our sixty-five pounds per day danger money paled into insignificance. What had seemed like an adrenaline rush and a bit of excitement back on the *Mokran* was now a frightening experience; life continuing at the role of the dice. It was almost certainly having grown older and more responsible, and almost certainly my forth-coming engagement, but the risks had become a very real, and the 'danger money' had become virtually irrelevant.

I recall being on the Bridge one hot sunny day, just playing 'day tripper', enjoying the cleanliness outside the engine room and the opportunity to stride around sight-seeing. There was an emergency call on channel 16 VHF by a stricken tanker, hit by an Iraqi missile. It sent a real chill down my spine: the panic-stricken voice of the watch-keeper with his ship in flames, exploding around him, colleagues killed. It focussed the mind.

This culminated in our ship being 'pinned down' for over a week, anchored off Lavan Island at the mouth of the Straits of Hormuz, being attacked regularly, praying our time wasn't up. My parents were being Telexed daily to confirm I was still alive.

We finally sailed to Singapore, where I paid off for the last time ever with BP Shipping (as it was then called).

I had decided this was to be my last trip. I had met Deidre and couldn't face another long trip like the previous two. BP had held high standards in terms of maintenance and innovation (inert gas systems, STORM units, fuel oil homogenisers etc) but standards had plummeted with agency manning, by bringing in far lower abilities and international communications: anything from difficult to "forget it". Changing watches had become a farce at times, with hand signs replacing verbal communication.

The Gulf War and constant threat of death (by now a real and understood risk) had ground me down; it was time to go. My long-term career had come to an abrupt and sorry end. I paid off in Singapore along with a few others who, like me, had had enough of the decline of the fleet and its foreign flag registration; its breaking up into three 'fleets', was the final straw.

I drowned my sorrows over a few Tigers (Singapore's local lager) and contemplated the future. I inadvertently caught the eye of a stunning girl sat the other side of the bar and we eventually got chatting. She seemed very interesting and we chatted for ages. I'm not proud of this, but she turned out to be a very sophisticated hooker and she'd spun her web. No need to expand on the situation or offer you the gory details, but it was a great night.

I woke the next morning feeling like shit. OK, my head wasn't quite clear, but the reality and enormity of what I'd done was like a tourniquet around my throat. I was going home and had no means of turning back time. I had done this sort of thing many times over the years (never in Europe – that's cheating) but never when I'd had a serious girlfriend, and I'd always had the chance to end the relationship before having sex on my return home. I'd have to Cum Clean.

With my tail between my legs and trepidation in my heart, I had to explain, praying I'd get away with my wayward stroll. Deidre was devastated but understanding and my pleas were met with a begrudging acceptance. This was to be a very effective lesson for me, which remained with me over the following years.

I paid off just before Christmas and Deidre and I became engaged between Christmas and New Year. Dad was dead chuffed for us. Announcing this to my mother was traumatic. Mum pointed out all the common-sense reasons not to do this. Her rationale was correct but I didn't want to hear it.

Shore leave was a short affair, four weeks as I recall. I was keen not to clock up too much UK-time, and to benefit from Maggie's tax dodge. Having to keep within strict parameters, I stuffed my money into an off-shore account and flew off abroad with my fiancée for a well-earned two-week holiday, keeping out of UK territory.

Coasters

I tried a brief period (very brief) working on two thousand-ton 'coasters' for a Medway-based shipping company. Oh my God, this was like a game after deep-sea with BP. I worked as relieving Second Engineer on the *Kinderence* and *Luminence*, there actually only being two engineers on board! The Chief Engineers were almost always too drunk to leave their cabins, let alone venture into the engine room.

These two ships were hell to work aboard; two thousand tons made these two ships the largest in the fleet! I seem to recall the smallest of the fleet was around seven hundred tons, basically a steel rowing boat. Most of the crew had 'done time', predominantly for ABH and/or GBH. When the crew went on the binge, it was time to make oneself scarce, lock the cabin door and 'play dead'.

Rank had little or no meaning, discipline was optional; most officers had little training and no qualifications. The worlds between coasting and BP were way too far apart for comparison of any type or meaning. The ships were clean enough, nicely painted, but the real maintenance was non-existent, and to a deep-sea engineer it was murder.

The fleet was general cargo tramp-steaming, and both ships had two one thousand-ton holds in which we would carry anything going, preferably for good profit. Our salaries were based on the profitability of the cargo, the entire crew earning a percentage of the profit. This was split between the crew with the highest percentage going to 'The Old Man', then reducing with rank and seniority. Thus, sitting in harbour waiting for rough seas to abate was a 'No-No', so we would carry anything from lodestone (gravel), to corn/wheat/seeds, to urea (powdered piss). Urea was a good cargo as it yielded high margins but it stank, the aroma wafting into the accommodation from the holds.

Obviously between cargoes, the holds would need cleaning out and this should have been done in port, tied up alongside. But because of the pressure to earn, the holds would be battened down and sealed and we'd potter off out of sight of land, open the hatches, clamber down into the holds, and hose them out using fire hoses, hoping wayward waves didn't lap up the minimal freeboard and slosh into the belly of the ship. Anyone who has read anything about the *Herald of Free Enterprise* will understand that 'free surface effect' is not a good thing. Having been lucky once again, and not capsized, the hatches would be battened down and we'd live to tell the tale.

These ships were coasters, quite literally going from port to port, hugging the coastline like a kid to its mother's apron strings. Once, having orders for the far-off port of La Coruna in the remote land of Spain, as our Captain wasn't qualified to master the ship, the ex-BP Second Mate was made responsible for the ship in Law. Scary but true.

Prior to my joining her, The *Luminence* had been to Dagenham, where the crew had gone ashore for the usual drink-fest and the ship had been allowed to settle on the muddy bottom as the tide ebbed. Unfortunately, the Second Engineer had dashed off to the pub with the crew, forgetting to stop the sea pumps. As the tide fell, the ship came to rest on the river bed and the silt was pumped around the entire sea water cooling system until completely blocking it, including all equipment, strainers etc. I heard this tale on 'Day One' of joining her. Once ready to set sail, I found machinery overheating, and myself unable to keep anything running long enough to limp out of port.

'Lucky me' had to strip down much of the machinery and dig out the solid silt, then dive to my cabin to continue to throw up until hitting the next port. Never before having been seasick, I spent these two trips manning the engine room in to, and out of, port and the rest of the time either asleep or talking to 'the Big White Telephone'.

I was astounded the first time I was asked about food preferences and learned that the crew members (not the officers) took turns to cook (no catering staff!) and went shopping for stores, collecting our 'vittles' in a shopping trolley or two! This really was a come-down from my previous experiences. Meals were taken together in the galley/dining room and dress code was 'anything goes'. One Captain (Pedro) was a fat, smelly, repugnant chap, who often came to meals in cut-off shorts and sandals; no top, just a big hairy gut hanging over the table edge. On hot days he stank; on cold days he stank.

Whilst chugging along the coast of France and Portugal, heading for Spain, the Telegraph rang out. This was completely unexpected 'so far away' from land, so I was immediately down to the engine room for manoeuvres. The Bridge watchkeeper had spotted a body floating upside down, bobbing on the sea's surface. The body must have been there for quite some time, as it was bloated and had clearly been a meal or two for hungry gulls.

We tried to haul the poor sod onboard but he fell apart as we took up the weight, so we had to leave the various parts in the sea, drifting off in different directions. It transpired that he had been a Spanish trawlerman who had fallen overboard a week or so earlier and had been lost at sea. I doubt his coffin contained all his parts.

I only managed two months of this torture, then decided enough was enough. I was losing weight, almost all meals being ejected the second we passed the sea wall at every port. We generally loaded the lodestone in Southern Ireland and rounding Land's End was purgatory. Never before, or since, have I suffered like this.

Those coasters were bloody awful, bouncing around at the slightest hint of a ripple. Not for me. . .

Coming Ashore

Having suffered the discomfort of coasters, and being discredited by seasickness, I joined the land-lubbers ashore. What a culture shock.

Life after the BP fleet was an out of body experience. In those days our parents' generation (apart from my dad) joined a company and retired from the same company some fifty-plus years later with a gold watch and it had never occurred to me that this was not my destiny.

It had been a real struggle years ago deciding whether I wanted to be a deck officer or an engineer officer. I'd had confused feelings about whether I saw myself as a dashing naval officer on the Bridge, in full uniform surveying the blue horizon, or alternatively, to be employable if/when I left the sea. Remarkably I'd been astute enough to choose the latter.

It was a great surprise to discover that land lubbers clearly had no idea what a marine engineer was, did, or what they could do. I struggled to find any form of employment ashore.

I interviewed for a job repairing fork lift trucks. "And have you ever worked on a fork lift truck before?" *Well no, but a fork lift truck is a frame holding batteries, electric-driven hydraulic pump, solenoid valves and rams.*

On various ships I'd had to repair faulty hydraulics many a time: hydraulic valve drives, and once had to rebuild a crane's hydraulic mechanism on one ship. These are the large cranes you see on every tanker halfway down the main deck and are for lifting the huge flexible hoses used to pump the cargo onboard and ashore. These structures are built to lift many tons at a time; surely a fork lift truck must be child's play?

I met this negative response possibly hundreds of times and was getting thoroughly despondent. Finally, I landed a job with Cloads, a small private yacht chandler on the Barbican in Plymouth. I was a 'yachtie' by then and loved working surrounded by tabernacles and salty stuff; however, this was never going to sustain my way of life, let alone pay for the upkeep on my yacht.

And then it happened. Income Tax Return time. How the hell did The Inland Revenue know I'd visited Sullom Voe? And how the hell could two days in the back of beyond cost me my year's tax-free status? This was disastrous. The previous tax year included my enhanced pay (in lieu of leave) and the accumulation of who knows how much war bonus; there were many periods of five days at sixty-five pounds a day.

The final bill was thousands; even my Dad, who'd been a Tax Consultant in a previous life, couldn't save me. I had to take out a large loan and get a real job.

Around this time, Deidre and I held a house-warming party, having just moved into our 'new' three-bedroom semi in Costa-del-Ivybridge. The party was great fun and a good time was had by all. The booze was flowing and there were games a-plenty.

My RN mate Dave was there; the age-old RN/MN rivalry kicked in. We were extremely competitive in our friendly rivalry, which ultimately led to me on the back of a chair, suspended by my gut, upside down, trying to pick up a matchbox with my teeth without touching the floor.

Fortunately I was pissed and so when I slipped off the chair back and my head hit the floor, face flat against my chest, I didn't feel the full force of the tendons across my back and shoulder blades snapping. The next day, not so good.

Deidre and I drove up to the RD&E hospital in Exeter to visit my younger sister Cathy, who was lying in a ward, hooked up to a drip-feed, totally dehydrated from a severe and threatening bout of the 'kissing disease'. Clearly, she'd kissed a poisonous frog? This was quite handy really as it wasn't too far for me to get down to A&E where I was x-rayed and had a neck brace fitted. I was in agony.

Obviously, I lost my job at Cloads, having managed to survive a full two weeks employment ashore.

Life Ashore

Life at sea had deteriorated beyond recognition from the early days. BP's seafarers had all been made redundant, their ships were then manned by agency staff, maintenance standards had plummeted and I had left to work on coasters; these were worse still - and I got seasick.

I initially ~~worked~~ was employed by the Department of the Environment Property Services Agency. This was like stepping onto the moon. Totally entrapped in red tape and bureaucracy, with most efforts being expended on making no effort; one guy sacked for sleeping in in a remote plantroom. It was as though DOE/PSA was managed by the French authorities. Thus, I moved on before my cerebellum jellified.

My first employment in an office environment was an eye-opener. I had a great relationship (totally platonic I might add) with the company's Receptionist. I recall once, we were enjoying a bit of banter and I threatened to put her over my knee and spank her if she repeated what she had said (I forget what this was). This she did, and this I did; it was just a laugh between consenting adults. The General Manager walked in just as I was administrating said punishment and all hell broke loose. How dull.

My career ashore has bounced around different parts of the construction industry: mechanical and electrical installation projects, maintenance, finally settling with BeMS (building control systems and energy management). In 1989 I 'fell' into construction and the office had a Fax machine. This was an absolutely incredible invention, and mystically sent words and pictures from one facsimile machine to another via a 'phone call'. I was blown away; until then I'd only ever had experience of visual communication by Telex. Now we have e-mail and attachments I can't imagine why anyone would need or want a fax machine.

I look back over my relatively short career at sea and wonder what more I could have packed into this period. I hope future generations will be able to look back and laugh at this small peep at life in the Seventies and Eighties, and not be too disgusted at our opinions and prejudices of the day. Fortunately, the world is gradually changing, but I am pleased to have experienced the rawness of earlier times, and see the dawning of our new age: that of enlightenment and acceptance.

It is sad that thirty-forty years ago, in an almost all-male environment, we lived and worked amongst 'gays' and cross-dressers, and this was never an issue, not discussed in any form of derogatory way. Political correctness has become so prevalent in our society at this time, and LGBT has become a minefield which is very sad, and such a quantum leap backwards in my mind.

I have written this book before the details have become vague and distorted in my memory. At times I miss the sea and my nautical career, but I like going home at night. Occasionally I dream of being back at sea, and a recurring worry is not having a clean boiler suit to wear on watch; most odd. I miss the comradery and the extremes of the responsibility when things go wrong, and the feeling of the wind in your hair as the ship ploughs through a balmy sea under blue skies.

This book is dedicated to my grandchildren, as yet unborn, as an insight to an earlier age, and the world that had not yet been cleansed and sterilised, when we could acknowledge that we are not sexless, colourless, all-accepting clones.

I hope you can enjoy this small slice of history too.

Acknowledgements

I would like to express my gratitude to the following people without whom this book would never have been written, each one of them offering their own unique assistance:

My wife, well, for being my wife and putting up with me.

My elder sister Karen, for helping with grammar and the formalities of the production of this memoir. Seriously, without her help and tenacity this book would not have happened.

My parents, for copulating at exactly the right moment to produce 'me'.

My dear friend, Rob West (deceased), who was part of so many 'wacky' episodes, and who experienced far more outrageous adventures than I ever did. At our last time together, we discussed the production of this book; he was extremely positive about the idea, reminding me of the great times we had enjoyed together over the previous thirty-six years.

God, for completing the world in only seven days, and giving 'us all creatures great and small'.

Charles Darwin, for giving us a touch of reality (see above).

The Romans, for giving us wine, public health, fresh water, irrigation, sanitation, street lighting, and prostitution. I'll forgive them the straight roads issue based on the fact that motorbikes were in their infancy. They had almost got sidecars right, with the invention of the chariot, but had yet to sort out the combustion engine.

Rudolf Diesel, for the internal combustion engine using adiabatic compression.

Edward Butler, for petrol-fuelled engine using adiabatic and isothermal heat transfers.

My Bank Manager, for allowing me ridiculous overdrafts following particularly good shore leaves. Oh! and my mother for negotiating this with him for me.

Boris Johnson and Donald Trump, for bringing mirth and merriment into politics.

Jeremy Corbyn, for disappearing into the sunset.

Alan Turing, for the invention of the personal computer; 'cut', 'copy', and 'paste' enabling me to invoke some logic into my meandering thoughts.

The Romans . . . .

Printed in Great Britain
by Amazon